ON
TELEVISION

ON
TELEVISION

PIERRE BOURDIEU

translated from the French
by Priscilla Parkhurst Ferguson

THE NEW PRESS

NEW YORK

The New Press is grateful for support of this publication from
the French Ministry of Culture.

Published in the United States by The New Press, New York, 1998
Distributed by W. W. Norton & Company, Inc., New York

LIBRARY OF CONGRESS CATALOGING-IN-PUBLICATION DATA

Bourdieu, Pierre.
    [Sur la télévision. English]
    On television / by Pierre Bourdieu; translated from
    the French by Priscilla Parkhurst Ferguson.
    p.   cm.
    Includes bibliographical references
    ISBN 1-56584-407-6 (hc.)
    ISBN 1-56584-512-9 (pbk.)
    1. Television broadcasting of news. 2. Television—
    Social aspects. 3. Journalism—Social aspects. I. Title.
    PN4884.T4B86   1998
    070.1′95—cd21   97–40535

The New Press was established in 1990 as a not-for-profit
alternative to the large, commercial publishing houses currently
dominating the book publishing industry. The New Press
operates in the public interest rather than for private gain, and is
committed to publishing, in innovative ways, works of
educational, cultural, and community value that are often
deemed insufficiently profitable.

The New Press
450 West 41st Street, 6th floor
New York, NY 10036

www.thenewpress.com

Printed in the United States of America

3 5 7 9 10 8 6 4 2

ON
TELEVISION

CONTENTS

PROLOGUE

Journalism and Politics

It should go without saying that to reveal the hidden constraints on journalists, which they in turn bring to bear on all cultural producers, is not to denounce those in charge or to point a finger at the guilty parties.[1] Rather, it is an attempt to offer to all sides a possibility of liberation, through a conscious effort, from the hold of these mechanisms, and to propose, perhaps, a program for concerted action by artists, writers, scholars, and journalists—that is, by the holders of the (quasi) monopoly of the instruments of diffusion. Only through such a collaboration will it be possible to work effectively to share the most universal achievements of research and to begin, in practical terms, to universalize the conditions of access to the universal.

What can possibly explain the remarkably violent reactions by so many of France's best-known journalists to this analysis?[2] Surely, with all my disavowals, they can't have felt personally targeted (at least the ones who were cited directly, or indirectly through people who work with them or who are like them). In part, no doubt, their virtuous indignation can be attributed to the *transcription effect*—the elimination by transcription of the nonverbal accompaniment to words such as tone, gestures, and mimicry. An impartial viewer perceives these elements, which make all the difference between a discussion meant to produce understanding and the polemic that most journalists saw in this book.

But the furor is best explained by certain attributes typical of the journalistic vision (the very characteristics that generated so much enthusiasm for a book such as *La Misère du monde* just a few years ago[3]): a tendency to equate what is new with what are usually called "revelations"; an emphasis on that which is most obvious in the social world, meaning individuals, what they do, and especially what they do wrong; and, finally, a readiness to denounce or indict. All of these inclinations hinder an understanding of the invisible structures and mechanisms (here, those of the journalistic field) that influence the actions and thoughts of individuals—an understanding that is likely to lead to sympathetic indulgence rather than to indignant condemnation. Then again, there is a predisposition to focus on an analyst's (supposed) "conclusions" rather than the method by which those conclusions were reached. After the publication of *The State Nobility: Elite Schools in the Field of Power*, the result and summing-up of ten years of my research, I remember vividly a journalist who proposed a debate on the Grandes Écoles: the president of the alumni association would speak "for" and I would speak "against."[4] And he hadn't a clue as to why I refused. In just the same way, the journalistic "big guns" who went after my book simply bracketed my method (in particular the analysis of journalism as a field); without even being aware of what they were doing, they reduced the book to a series of utterly hackneyed positions punctuated by a smattering of polemical outbursts.

But this method is precisely what I want to come back to. Even at the risk of new misunderstandings, I want to try to show how the journalistic field produces and imposes on the public a very particular vision of the political field, a vision that is grounded in the very structure of the journalistic field and in journalists' specific interests produced in and by that field.

In a world ruled by the fear of being boring and anxiety about being amusing at all costs, politics is bound to be unappealing, better kept out of prime time as much as possible. So, insofar as it does have to be addressed, this not very exciting and even depressing spectacle, which is so difficult to deal with, has to be made interesting. This imperative explains why, in the United States as much as in Europe, there is a tendency to shunt aside serious commentators and investigative reporters in favor of the talk show host. It also explains why real information, analysis, in-depth interviews, expert discussions, and serious documentaries lose out to pure entertainment and, in particular, to mindless talk show chatter between "approved" and interchangeable speakers. (In the text that follows, I seem to have committed the unpardonable sin of mentioning a couple of them as examples). To understand what is said in these staged "exchanges" and, in particular, what *can* be said, would require a detailed analysis of the selection process for these individuals, whom Americans call "panelists." These people are always available—meaning always ready not merely to participate but to play the game— and they answer all the questions journalists ask, no matter how silly or outrageous. They're ready for everything and anything, which means to make any concession (as to the subject under discussion, the other participants, and so on), any compromise, any deal as long as they can be "in" on things and receive the direct and indirect benefits of "media" celebrity— prestige in the media world, big fees on the lecture circuit, and so on. Further, particularly at the pre-interviews conducted by some producers in the United States and increasingly in Europe as well, prospective panelists must present their positions in uncomplicated, clear, and striking terms. Above all, they must avoid the quagmire of intellectual complexity. (As the maxim goes, "The less you know, the better off you are.")

To justify this policy of demagogic simplification (which is absolutely and utterly contrary to the democratic goal of informing or educating people by interesting them), journalists point to the public's expectations. But in fact they are projecting onto the public their own inclinations and their own views. Because they're so afraid of being boring, they opt for confrontations over debates, prefer polemics over rigorous argument, and in general, do whatever they can to promote conflict. They prefer to confront individuals (politicians in particular) instead of confronting their arguments, that is, what's really at stake in the debate, whether the budget deficit, taxes, or the balance of trade. Given that their claims to competence are based more on their claims to close contacts in the political realm, including access to insider information (even rumors and malicious gossip), than on the objectivity of their observation and investigation, journalists like to stick to their home territory. They direct attention to the game and its players rather than to what is really at stake, because these are the sources of their interest and expertise. They are more interested in the tactics of politics than in the substance, and more concerned with the political effect of speeches and politicians' maneuverings within the political field (in terms of coalitions, alliances, or individual conflicts) than with the meaning of these. (That is, when they don't simply invent issues, such as the question during the 1997 French elections of whether the contest between the Left and the Right was going to take place between two main contenders—Lionel Jospin, leader of the Socialist opposition, and Alain Juppé, the conservative prime minister—or between four politicians—Jospin and Robert Hue, his Communist ally, on one side, and, on the other, Juppé and his centrist ally, François Léotard. Despite its apparent neutrality, the emphasis given to this question actually made an overtly political move in favor of the conservatives by focusing attention on possible splits on the left, between the leading candidate Jospin and his minor, Communist ally.)

Journalists occupy an ambiguous position in the political world, in which they are very influential actors but not full-fledged members. This position enables them to offer politicians vital symbolic support that they can't get for themselves. (Except, today, collectively, in publishing, where cronyism ensures favorable reviews for journalists and their books). This means that journalists are apt to look at things rather like Thersites, the ugly, cowardly, "thrower of words" in the *Iliad*, who abuses everybody and "argues nothing but scandal."[5]

Typically they adopt a spontaneous form of a philosophy of doubt, which leads them to ascribe the sincerest convictions and most disinterested political positions to interests tied to particular positions within the political field (such as rivalries within a party, or participation in a "trend").

All of this leads them to a cynical view of politics, which is reflected in their political arguments, and in their interview questions. For them, politics becomes an arena full of hyper-ambitious people with no convictions but with a clear sense of the competitive situation and of their opposing interests. (Journalists are certainly encouraged in this attitude by political consultants and advisers, who help politicians with this sort of explicitly calculated, though not necessarily cynical, kind of political marketing. Political success increasingly depends on adapting to the demands of the journalistic field, which becomes a "caucus" increasingly responsible for "making" both politicians and their reputations.) This exclusive attention to the political "microcosm" and to the facts and effects that can be attributed to it, tends to produce a break with the public, or at least with those segments of the public most concerned with the real consequences of these political positions on their lives and on society at large. This break is duplicated and greatly reinforced, particularly in the case of journalism's big television stars, by the social distance that comes with high economic and social status. It is common knowledge that, since the 1960s, in the United States and in most of Europe, media stars augment their already high salaries—on the order of $100,000 and more in Europe, and several million dollars on the American side[6]—with often-exorbitant honoraria for talk show appearances and lectures, remuneration for regular newspaper collaboration, and fees from various "deals," notably at annual conventions and professional meetings. This is why we see the continuing increase in the distribution of power and privilege in the journalistic field. Some journalists act much like small-time capitalistic entrepreneurs who need to preserve, and increase, their symbolic capital—since their me-

dia visibility increases their value on the lecture circuit. At the
same time, we are witnessing the growth of a vast journalistic
subproletariat, forced into a kind of self-censorship by an increasingly precarious job situation.[7]

To these effects must be added others, on which I will elaborate in this book, that derive from competition within the journalistic field itself—the obsession with "scoops" and the
unquestioned bias in favor of the news that is the newest and
hardest to get; or the predisposition to overstatement that
comes from attempting to offer the subtlest and strangest in-
terpretation (which often means the most cynical one); or
again, the predictions game, made possible by a collective amnesia about current events. Not only are these predictions and
diagnoses easy to make (like bets on sports events) but they can
be made with total impunity, protected as the predictor is by
the rapidity with which the journalistic report is forgotten
amid the rapid turnover of events. (This amnesia explains how,
in the space of a few months in 1989, journalists the world
over switched from exalting the dazzling emergence of new
democracies to condemning the appalling ethnic wars).

These mechanisms work in concert to produce a general
effect of depoliticization or, more precisely, disenchantment
with politics. Nothing need be said about current events, since
whenever politics raises an important but unmistakably boring
question, the search for entertainment focuses attention on a
spectacle (or a scandal) every time. "Current events" are reduced to an impassioned recital of entertaining events, which
tend to lie about halfway between the human interest story and
the variety show. (For an exemplary case, take the O. J. Simpson trial.) The result is a litany of events with no beginning
and no real end, thrown together only because they occurred at
the same time. So an earthquake in Turkey turns up next to
proposed budget cuts, and a championship sports team is fea-
tured alongside a big murder trial. These events are reduced to
the level of the absurd because we see only those elements that
can be shown on television at a given moment, cut off from

their antecedents and consequences. There is a patent lack of interest in subtle, nuanced changes, or in processes that, like the continental drift, remain unperceived and imperceptible in the moment, revealing their effects only in the long term. This inattention to nuance both repeats and reinforces the structural amnesia induced by day-to-day thinking and by the competition that equates what's important with what's new—the scoop. This means that journalists—the day laborers of everyday life—can show us the world only as a series of unrelated flash photos. Given the lack of time, and especially the lack of interest and information (research and documentation are usually confined to reading articles that have appeared in the press), they cannot do what would be necessary to make events (say, an outbreak of violence in a high school) really understandable, that is, they cannot reinsert them in a network of relevant relationships (such as the family structure, which is tied to the job market, itself tied to governmental hiring policies, and so on). No doubt, they are encouraged to act as they do by politicians, and especially by government officials (who are in turn encouraged by the politicians), both of whom like to stress the short-term effects of the decisions they make and announce to the public. Clearly, these dramatic "coups" they favor create a climate hostile to action whose effect is visible only over time.

This vision is at once dehistoricized and dehistoricizing, fragmented and fragmenting. Its paradigmatic expression is the TV news and the way it sees the world—as a series of apparently absurd stories that all end up looking the same, endless parades of poverty-stricken countries, sequences of events that, having appeared with no explanation, will disappear with no solution—Zaire today, Bosnia yesterday, the Congo tomorrow. Stripped of any political necessity, this string of events can at best arouse a vague humanitarian interest. Coming one after the other and outside any historical perspective, these unconnected tragedies seem to differ little from natural disasters—the tornadoes, forest fires, and floods that also occupy so much of the news. It's almost a journalistic ritual, and certainly a tradition, to focus on simple events that are simple to cover. As for the victims, they're not presented in any more political a light than those of a train derailment or any other accident. We see nothing that might stimulate any sort of truly political cohesion or revolt.

So, especially as a result of the particular form that competition takes there, and through the routines and habits of thought it imposes, the journalistic field represents the world in terms of a philosophy that sees history as an absurd series of disasters which can be neither understood nor influenced. Journalism shows us a world full of ethnic wars, racist hatred, violence and crime—a world full of incomprehensible and unsettling dangers from which we must withdraw for our own protection. And when its commentators spew ethnocentric or racist contempt (as they often do, especially whenever Africa or the inner city are involved), the journalistic evocation of the world does not serve to mobilize or politicize; on the contrary, it only increases xenophobic fears, just as the delusion that crime and violence are always and everywhere on the rise feeds anxieties and phobias about safety in the streets and at home. The world shown by television is one that lies beyond the grasp of ordinary individuals. Linked to this is the impression that politics is for professionals, a bit like high-level competitive sports with their split between athletes and spectators. Especially among those who are basically apolitical, this worldview fosters fatalism and disengagement, which obviously favors the status quo. It requires blind faith in ordinary individuals' (undeniable but limited) capacity for "resistance" to assume, along with a certain "postmodern cultural criticism," that television viewers' active cynicism (exemplified by channel surfing) can do much to counter the cynicism of its producers, whose mindset, working conditions, and goals—reaching the biggest public with that "extra something" that "sells"—make them more and more like advertising people. Facility with the games of cultural criticism—their "I know that you know that I know"—is not universal. Nor is the ability to spin out elaborate "readings" of the "ironic and metatextual" messages cynically manipulated by television producers and ad people. Anyone who thinks otherwise has simply surrendered to a populist version of one of the most perverse forms of academic pedantry.

ON TELEVISION[1]

PREFACE

I decided to give these two lectures on television because I wanted to reach beyond the usual audience at the Collège de France. I think that television poses a serious danger for all the various areas of cultural production—for art, for literature, for science, for philosophy, and for law. What's more, contrary to what a lot of journalists—even the most responsible of them—say (and think), undoubtedly in all good faith, I think that television poses no less of a threat to political life and to democracy itself. I shall try to explain these views rapidly—a systematic, in-depth analysis would have taken much more time. I could prove this claim easily. I could analyze how, precisely because its goal is the largest audience possible, television, along with some print journalism, has treated individuals who make jingoistic or racist statements, and/or act accordingly. Then again, I could simply run through all the compromises television makes every day with a narrow and narrowly national, not to say chauvinistic, vision of politics. And lest I be accused of fixing on a situation that is strictly French, I'll remind you of the media's treatment of the O. J. Simpson trial, and of a more recent case in which an ordinary murder got turned into a "sex crime" and brought on a whole series of uncontrollable legal consequences.

But it is a recent if less well-known incident between Greece and Turkey that best illustrates the real dangers that come from the relentless competition for an ever-larger audience share. After a private TV station in Greece issued all kinds of calls to action and belligerent statements about the tiny deserted island of Imia, private radio and television in Greece, egged on by the print media, worked themselves into a nationalistic frenzy. Carried along by the same battle for audience ratings, Turkish TV and newspapers jumped on the bandwagon. Greek soldiers landed on the island, the two fleets moved into position—and war was only just avoided. The key to what is really new in these nationalistic outbursts—in Turkey and Greece, but also in the former Yugoslavia, in France and elsewhere—may well lie in the ways modern media are able to exploit these primal passions.

To keep the promise that I had made to myself about this lecture, which I conceived as an *exchange* within a larger debate, I had to construct my arguments so that they would be clear to everyone. This meant, in more than one instance, that I had to simplify or make do with approximations. To maintain the focus on the crucial element—the lecture itself—and contrary to what usually happens on television I chose, in agreement with the producer, to eliminate effects such as changes in the format or camera angles. I also left out illustrations (selections from broadcasts, reproductions of documents, statistics, and so on). Besides taking up precious time, all of these things undoubtedly would have made it harder to follow my argument. The contrast with regular television—the object of the analysis—was, by design, a way of affirming the independence of analytical and critical discourse, even in the cumbersome, didactic, and dogmatic guise of a large public lecture. Television has gradually done away with this kind of discourse (political debates in the United States are said to allow no one to speak for more than seven seconds). But intellectual discourse remains one of the most authentic forms of resistance to manipulation and a vital affirmation of the freedom of thought.

I am well aware that this sort of talk is only a makeshift solution, a less effective and less amusing substitute for a true critique of images through images—of the sort you find in some of Jean-Luc Godard's films, for example or those of Pierre Carles. I also know that what I am doing continues, or complements, the constant battle of all professionals who work with images and fight for "the independence of their communication code." I am thinking in particular of the critical reflection on images of which Jean-Luc Godard (once again) gives an exemplary illustration in his analysis of the uses made of the journalist Joseph Kraft's photograph of Jane Fonda in North Vietnam. Indeed, I could have taken Godard's agenda as my own: "This work was a beginning of a political [I would say sociological] questioning of images and sounds, and of their *relations*. It meant no longer saying, 'That's a just image' but 'That's just an image'; no longer saying, 'That's a Union officer on a horse,' but, 'That's an *image* of a horse and an officer.' "[2]

Though I don't harbor many illusions on this score, I can hope that my analysis will not be taken as an "attack" on journalists and television stemming from some sort of nostalgia for the supposed good old days of cultural television, TV-Sorbonne style, or as a refusal—equally reactive and regressive—of everything that television truly can contribute, whatever its faults (certain documentaries, for example). Even though I have every reason to fear that this discussion will mostly feed into the narcissistic complacency of a journalistic world all too inclined to pseudo-criticism, I hope that it will furnish some tools or weapons to all those in the image professions who are struggling to keep what could have become an extraordinary instrument of direct democracy from turning into an instrument of symbolic oppression.

PART ONE

In Front of the Camera and Behind the Scenes

I'd like to try and pose here, on television, a certain number of questions about television. This is a bit paradoxical since, in general, I think that you can't say much on television, particularly not about television. But if it's true that you can't say anything on television, shouldn't I join a certain number of our top intellectuals, artists, and writers and conclude that one should simply steer clear of it?

It seems to me that we don't have to accept this alternative. I think that it is important to talk on television *under certain conditions*. Today, thanks to the audiovisual services of the Collège de France, I am speaking under absolutely exceptional circumstances. In the first place, I face no time limit; second, my topic is my own, not one imposed on me (I was free to choose whatever topic I wanted and I can still change it); and, third, there is nobody here, as for regular programs, to bring me into line with technical requirements, with the "public-that-won't-understand," with morality or decency, or with whatever else. The situation is absolutely unique because, to use out-of-date terms, I have a *control of the instruments of production* which is not at all usual. The fact that these conditions are exceptional in itself says something about what usually happens when someone appears on television.

But, you may well ask, why do people accept such conditions? That's a very important question, and, further, one not asked by most of the researchers, scholars, and writers—not to mention journalists—who appear on television. We need to question this failure to ask questions. In fact, it seems to me that, by agreeing to appear on television shows without worrying about whether you'll be able to say anything, you make it very clear that you're not there to say anything at all but for altogether different reasons, chief among them the desire to be seen. Berkeley said that "to be is to be perceived." For some of our thinkers (and our writers), to be is to be perceived on television, which means, when all is said and done, to be perceived by journalists, to be, as the saying goes, on their "good side," with all the compromises and concessions that implies. And it is certainly true that, since they can hardly count on having their work last over time, they have no recourse but to appear on television as often as possible. This means churning out regularly and as often as possible works whose principal function, as Gilles Deleuze used to say, is to get them on television. So the television screen today becomes a sort of mirror for Narcissus, a space for narcissistic exhibitionism.

This preamble may seem a bit long, but it appears to me desirable that artists, writers, and thinkers ask themselves these questions. This should be done openly and collectively, if possible, so that no one is left alone with the decision of whether or not to appear on television, and, if appearing, of whether to stipulate conditions. What I'd really like (you can always dream) is for them to set up collective negotiations with journalists toward some sort of a contract. It goes without saying that it is not a question of blaming or fighting journalists, who often suffer a good deal from the very constraints they are forced to impose. On the contrary, it's to try to see how we can work together to overcome the threat of instrumentalization.

I don't think you can refuse categorically to talk on television. In certain cases, there can even be something of a *duty* to do so, again under the right conditions. In making this choice, one must take into account the specificities of television. With television, we are dealing with an instrument that offers, theoretically, the possibility of reaching everybody. This brings up a number of questions. Is what I have to say meant to reach everybody? Am I ready to make what I say understandable by everybody? Is it worth being understood by everybody? You can go even further: should it be understood by everybody? Researchers, and scholars in particular, have an obligation— and it may be especially urgent for the social sciences—to make the advances of research available to everyone. In Europe, at least, we are, as Edmund Husserl used to say, "humanity's civil servants," paid by the government to make discoveries, either about the natural world or about the social world. It seems to me that part of our responsibility is to share what we have found. I have always tried to ask myself these questions before deciding whether or not to agree to public appearances. These are questions that I would like everyone invited to appear on television to pose or be forced to pose because the television audience and the television critics pose them: Do I have something to say? Can I say it in these conditions? Is what I have to say worth saying here and now? In a word, what am I doing here?

INVISIBLE CENSORSHIP

But let me return to the essential point. I began by claiming that open access to television is offset by a powerful censorship, a loss of independence linked to the conditions imposed on those who speak on television. Above all, time limits make it highly unlikely that anything can be said. I am undoubtedly expected to say that this television censorship—of guests but also of the journalists who are its agents—is political. It's true that politics intervenes, and that there is political control (particularly in the case of hiring for top positions in the radio stations and television channels under direct government control). It is also true that at a time such as today, when great numbers of people are looking for work and there is so little job security in television and radio, there is a greater tendency toward political conformity. Consciously or unconsciously, people censor themselves—they don't need to be called into line.

You can also consider economic censorship. It is true that, in the final analysis, you can say that the pressure on television is economic. That said, it is not enough to say that what gets on television is determined by the owners, by the companies that pay for the ads, or by the government that gives the subsidies. If you knew only the name of the owner of a television station, its advertising budget, and how much it receives in subsidies, you wouldn't know much. Still, it's important to keep these things in mind. It's important to know that NBC is owned by General Electric (which means that interviews with people who live near a nuclear plant undoubtedly would be . . . but then again, such a story wouldn't even occur to anyone), that CBS is owned by Westinghouse, and ABC by Disney, that TF1 belongs to Bouygues[1], and that these facts lead to consequences through a whole series of mediations. It is obvious that the government won't do certain things to Bouygues, knowing that Bouygues is behind TF1. These factors, which are so crude that they are obvious to even the most simple-minded critique, hide other things, all the anonymous and invisible mechanisms through which the many kinds of censorship operate to make television such a formidable instrument for maintaining the symbolic order.

I'd like to pause here. Sociological analysis often comes up against a misconception. Anyone involved as the object of the analysis, in this case journalists, tends to think that the work of analysis, the revelation of mechanisms, is in fact a denunciation of individuals, part of an ad hominem polemic. (Those same journalists would, of course, immediately level accusations of bias and lack of objectivity at any sociologist who discussed or wrote about even a tenth of what comes up anytime you talk with the media about the payoffs, how the programs are manufactured, made up—that's the word they use.) In general, people don't like to be turned into objects or objectified, and journalists least of all. They feel under fire, singled out. But the further you get in the analysis of a given milieu, the more likely you are to let individuals off the hook (which doesn't mean justifying everything that happens). And the more you understand how things work, the more you come to understand that the people involved are manipulated as much as they manipulate. They manipulate even more effectively the more they are themselves manipulated and the more unconscious they are of this.

I stress this point even though I know that, whatever I do, anything I say will be taken as a criticism—a reaction that is also a defense against analysis. But let me stress that I even think that scandals such as the furor over the deeds and misdeeds of one or another television news personality, or the exorbitant salaries of certain producers, divert attention from the main point. Individual corruption only masks the *structural corruption* (should we even talk about corruption in this case?) that operates on the game as a whole through mechanisms such as competition for market share. This is what I want to examine.

So I would like to analyze a series of mechanisms that allow television to wield a particularly pernicious form of symbolic violence. Symbolic violence is violence wielded with tacit complicity between its victims and its agents, insofar as both remain unconscious of submitting to or wielding it. The function of sociology, as of every science, is to reveal that which is hidden. In so doing, it can help minimize the symbolic violence within social relations and, in particular, within the relations of communication.

Let's start with an easy example—sensational news. This has always been the favorite food of the tabloids. Blood, sex, melodrama and crime have always been big sellers. In the early days of television, a sense of respectability modeled on the printed press kept these attention-grabbers under wraps, but the race for audience share inevitably brings it to the headlines and to the beginning of the television news. Sensationalism attracts notice, and it also diverts it, like magicians whose basic operating principle is to direct attention to something other than what they're doing. Part of the symbolic functioning of television, in the case of the news, for example, is to call attention to those elements which will engage everybody— which offer something for everyone. These are things that won't shock anyone, where nothing is at stake, that don't divide, are generally agreed on, and interest everybody without touching on anything important. These items are basic ingredients of news because they interest everyone, and because they take up time—time that could be used to say something else.

And time, on television, is an extremely rare commodity. When you use up precious time to say banal things, to the extent that they cover up precious things, these banalities become in fact very important. If I stress this point, it's because everyone knows that a very high proportion of the population reads no newspaper at all and is dependent on television as their sole source of news. Television enjoys a de facto monopoly on what goes into the heads of a significant part of the population and what they think. So much emphasis on headlines and so much filling up of precious time with empty air— with nothing or almost nothing—shunts aside relevant news, that is, the information that all citizens ought to have in order to exercise their democratic rights. We are therefore faced with a division, as far as news is concerned, between individuals in a position to read so-called "serious" newspapers (insofar as they can remain serious in the face of competition from television), and people with access to international newspapers and foreign radio stations, and, on the other hand, everyone else, who get from television news all they know about politics. That is to say, precious little, except for what can be learned from seeing people, how they look, and how they talk—things even the most culturally disadvantaged can decipher, and which can do more than a little to distance many of them from a good many politicians.

SHOW AND HIDE

So far I've emphasized elements that are easy to see. I'd like now to move on to slightly less obvious matters in order to show how, paradoxically, television can hide by showing. That is, it can hide things by showing something other than what would be shown if television did what it's supposed to do, provide information. Or by showing what has to be shown, but in such a way that it isn't really shown, or is turned into something insignificant; or by constructing it in such a way that it takes on a meaning that has nothing at all to do with reality.

On this point I'll take two examples from Patrick Champagne's work. In his work in *La Misère du monde*, Champagne offers a detailed examination of how the media represent events in the "inner city."[2] He shows how journalists are carried along by the inherent exigencies of their job, by their view of the world, by their training and orientation, and also by the reasoning intrinsic to the profession itself. They select very specific aspects of the inner city as a function of their particular perceptual categories, the particular way they see things. These categories are the product of education, history, and so forth. The most common metaphor to explain this notion of category—that is, the invisible structures that organize perception and determine what we see and don't see—is eyeglasses. Journalists have special "glasses" through which they see certain things and not others, and through which they see the things they see in the special way they see them.

The principle that determines this selection is the search for the sensational and the spectacular. Television calls for *dramatization*, in both senses of the term: it puts an event on stage, puts it in images. In doing so, it exaggerates the importance of that event, its seriousness, and its dramatic, even tragic character. For the inner city, this means riots. That's already a big word . . . And, indeed, words get the same treatment. Ordinary words impress no one, but paradoxically, the world of images is dominated by words. Photos are nothing without words—the French term for the caption is *legend*, and often they should be read as just that, as legends that can show anything at all. We know that to name is to show, to create, to bring into existence. And words can do a lot of damage: Islam, Islamic, Islamicist—is the headscarf Islamic or Islamicist?[3] And if it were really only a kerchief and *nothing more?* Sometimes I want to go back over *every* word the television newspeople use, often without thinking and with no idea of the difficulty and the seriousness of the subjects they are talking about or the responsibilities they assume by talking about them in front of the thousands of people who watch the news without understanding what they see and without understanding that they don't understand. Because these words do things, they make things—they create phantasms, fears, and phobias, or simply false representations.

Journalists, on the whole, are interested in the exception, which means whatever is exceptional *for them.* Something that might be perfectly ordinary for someone else can be extrordinary for them and vice versa. They're interested in the extraordinary, in anything that breaks the routine. The daily papers are under pressure to offer a daily dose of the extra-daily, and that's not easy . . . This pressure explains the attention they give to extraordinary occurrences, usual unusual events like fires, floods, or murders. But the extra-ordinary is also, and especially, what isn't ordinary for other newspapers. It's what differs from the ordinary and what differs from what other newspapers say. The pressure is dreadful—the pressure to get a "scoop."[4] People are ready to do almost anything to be the first to see and present something. The result is that everyone copies each other in the attempt to get ahead; everyone ends up doing the same thing. The search for exclusivity, which elsewhere leads to originality and singularity, here yields uniformity and banality.

This relentless, self-interested search for the extra-ordinary can have just as much political effect as direct political prescription or the self-censorship that comes from fear of being left behind or left out. With the exceptional force of the televised image at their disposal, journalists can produce effects that are literally incomparable. The monotonous, drab daily life in the inner city doesn't say anything to anybody and doesn't interest anybody, journalists least of all. But even if they were to take a real interest in what goes on in the inner city and really wanted to show it, it would be enormously difficult. There is nothing more difficult to convey than reality in all its ordinariness. Flaubert was fond of saying that it takes a lot of hard work to portray mediocrity. Sociologists run into this problem all the time: How can we make the ordinary extraordinary and evoke ordinariness in such a way that people will see just how extraordinary it is?

The political dangers inherent in the ordinary use of television have to do with the fact that images have the peculiar capacity to produce what literary critics call a *reality effect*. They show things and make people believe in what they show. This power to show is also a power to mobilize. It can give a life to ideas or images, but also to groups. The news, the incidents and accidents of everyday life, can be loaded with political or ethnic significance liable to unleash strong, often negative feelings, such as racism, chauvinism, the fear–hatred of the foreigner or, xenophobia. The simple report, the very fact of reporting, of *putting on record* as a reporter, always implies a social construction of reality that can mobilize (or demobilize) individuals or groups.

Another example from Patrick Champagne's work is the 1986 high school student strike. Here you see how journalists acting in all good faith and in complete innocence—merely letting themselves be guided by their interests (meaning what interests them), presuppositions, categories of perception and evaluation, and unconscious expectations—still produce reality effects and effects in reality. Nobody wants these effects, which, in certain cases, can be catastrophic. Journalists had in mind the political upheaval of May 1968 and were afraid of missing "a new 1968." Since they were dealing with teenagers who were not very politically aware and who had little idea of what to say, reporters went in search of articulate representatives or delegates (no doubt from among the most highly politicized).

Such commentators are taken seriously and take themselves seriously. One thing leads to another, and, ultimately television, which claims to record reality, creates it instead. We are getting closer and closer to the point where the social world is primarily described—and in a sense prescribed—by television. Let's suppose that I want to lobby for retirement at age fifty. A few years ago, I would have worked up a demonstration in Paris, there'd have been posters and a parade, and we'd have all marched over to the Ministry of National Education. Today—this is just barely an exaggeration—I'd need a savvy media consultant. With a few mediagenic elements to get attention—disguises, masks, whatever—television can produce an effect close to what you'd have from fifty thousand protesters in the streets.

At stake today in local as well as global political struggles is the capacity to impose a way of seeing the world, of making people wear "glasses" that force them to see the world divided up in certain ways (the young and the old, foreigners and the French . . .). These divisions create groups that can be mobilized, and that mobilization makes it possible for them to convince everyone else that they exist, to exert pressure and obtain privileges, and so forth. Television plays a determining role in all such struggles today. Anyone who still believes that you can organize a political demonstration without paying attention to television risks being left behind. It's more and more the case that you have to produce demonstrations for television so that they interest television types and fit their perceptual categories. Then, and only then, relayed and amplified by these television professionals, will your demonstration have its maximum effect.

THE CIRCULAR CIRCULATION OF INFORMATION

Until now, I've been talking as if the individual journalist were the subject of all these processes. But "the journalist" is an abstract entity that doesn't exist. What exists are journalists who differ by sex, age, level of education, affiliation, and "medium." The journalistic world is a divided one, full of conflict, competition, and rivalries. That said, my analysis remains valid in that journalistic *products* are much more alike than is generally thought. The most obvious differences, notably the political tendencies of the newspapers—which, in any case, it has to be said, are becoming less and less evident . . . —hide the profound similarities. These are traceable to the pressures imposed by sources and by a whole series of mechanisms, the most important of which is competition. Free market economics holds that monopoly creates uniformity and competition produces diversity. Obviously, I have nothing against competition, but I observe that competition homogenizes when it occurs between journalists or newspapers subject to identical pressures and opinion polls, and with the same basic cast of commentators (note how easily journalists move from one news medium or program to another). Just compare the weekly newsmagazine covers at two-week intervals and you'll find nearly identical headlines. Or again, in the case of a major network radio or television news, at best (or at worst) the order in which the news is presented is different.

This is due partly to the fact that production is a collective enterprise. In the cinema, for example, films are clearly the collective products of the individuals listed in the credits. But the collectivity that produces television messages can't be understood only as the group that puts a program together, because, as we have seen, it encompasses journalists as a whole. We always want to know who the subject of a discourse is, but here no one can ever be sure of being the subject of what is said . . . We're a lot less original than we think we are. This is particularly true where collective pressures, and particularly competitive pressures, are so strong that one is led to do things that one wouldn't do if the others didn't exist (in order, for example, to be first). No one reads as many newspapers as journalists, who tend to think that everybody reads all the newspapers (they forget, first of all, that lots of people read no paper at all, and second, that those who do read read only one. Unless you're in the profession, you don't often read *Le Monde, Le Figaro,* and *Libération* in the same day). For journalists a daily review of the press is an essential tool. To know what to say, you have to know what everyone else has said. This is one of the mechanisms that renders journalistic products so similar. If *Libération* gives headlines to a given event, *Le Monde* can't remain indifferent, although, given its particular prestige, it has the option of standing a bit apart in order to mark its distance and keep its reputation for being serious and aloof. But such tiny differences, to which journalists attach great importance, hide enormous similarities. Editorial staff spend a good deal of time talking about other newspapers, particularly about "what they did and we didn't do" ("we really blew that one") and what should have been done (no discussion on that point)—since the other paper did it. This dynamic is probably even more obvious for literature, art, or film criticism. If X talks about a book in *Libération*, Y will have to talk about it in *Le Monde* or *Le Nouvel Observateur* even if he considers it worthless or unimportant. And vice versa. This is the way media success is produced, and sometimes as well (but not always) commercial success.

This sort of game of mirrors reflecting one another produces a formidable effect of mental closure. Another example of this becomes clear in interviews with journalists: to put together the television news at noon, you have to have seen the headlines of the eight o'clock news the previous evening as well as the daily papers; to put together the headlines for the evening news, you must have read the morning papers. These are the tacit requirements of the job—to be up on things and to set yourself apart, often by tiny differences accorded fantastic importance by journalists and quite missed by the viewer. (This is an effect typical of the field: you do things for competitors that you think you're doing for consumers). For example, journalists will say—and this is a direct quote—"we left TF1 in the dust." This is a way of saying that they are competitors who direct much of their effort toward being different from one another. "We left TF1 in the dust" means that these differences are meaningful: "they didn't have the sound, and we did." These differences completely bypass the average viewer, who could perceive them only by watching several networks at the same time. But these differences, which go completely unnoticed by viewers, turn out to be very important for producers, who think that they are not only seen but boost ratings. Here is the hidden god of this universe who governs conduct and consciences. A one-point drop in audience ratings, can, in certain cases, mean instant death with no appeal. This is only one of the equations—incorrect in my view—made between program content and its supposed effect.

In some sense, the choices made on television are choices made by no subject. To explain this proposition, which may appear somewhat excessive, let me point simply to another of the effects of the circular circulation to which I referred above: the fact that journalists—who in any case have much in common, profession of course, but also social origin and education—meet one another daily in debates that always feature the same cast of characters. All of which produces the closure that I mentioned earlier, and also—no two ways about it—censorship. This censorship is as effective—more even, because its principle remains invisible—as direct political intervention from a central administration. To measure the closing-down effect of this vicious informational circle, just try programming some unscheduled news, events in Algeria or the status of foreigners in France, for example. Press conferences or releases on these subjects are useless; they are supposed to bore everyone, and it is impossible to get analysis of them into a newspaper unless it is written by someone with a big name—

that's what sells. You can only break out of the circle by breaking and entering, so to speak. But you can only break and enter through the media. You have to grab the attention of the media, or at least one "medium," so that the story can be picked up and amplified by its competitors.

If you wonder how the people in charge of giving us information get their own information, it appears that, in general, they get it from other informers. Of course, there's Agence France Presse or Associated Press, and there are agencies and official sources of information (government officials, the police, and so on) with which journalists necessarily enter into very complex relationships of exchange. But the really determining share of information, that is, the *information about information* that allows you to decide what is important and therefore worth broadcasting, comes in large part from other informers. This leads to a sort of leveling, a homogenization of standards. I remember one interview with a program executive for whom everything was absolutely obvious. When I asked him why he scheduled one item before another, his reply was, simply, "It's obvious." This is undoubtedly the reason that he had the job he had: his way of seeing things was perfectly adapted to the objective exigencies of his position. Of course, occupying as they do different positions within journalism, different journalists are less likely to find obvious what he found so obvious. The executives who worship at the altar of audience ratings have a feeling of "obviousness" which is not necessarily shared by the freelancer who proposes a topic only to be told that it's "not interesting." The journalistic milieu cannot be represented as uniform. There are small fry, newcomers, subversives, pains-in-the-neck who struggle desperately to add some small difference to this enormous, homogeneous mishmash imposed by the (vicious) circle of information circulating in a circle between people who—and this you can't forget—are all subject to audience ratings. Even network executives are ultimately slaves to the ratings.

Audience ratings—Nielsen ratings in the U.S.—measure the

audience share won by each network. It is now possible to pinpoint the audience by the quarter hour and even—a new development—by social group. So we know very precisely who's watching what, and who not. Even in the most independent sectors of journalism, ratings have become the journalist's Last Judgment, Aside from *Le Canard enchaîné* [a satirical weekly], *Le Monde diplomatique* [a distinguished, left liberal journal similar to *Foreign Affairs*], and a few small avant-garde journals supported by generous people who take their "irresponsibilities" seriously, everyone is fixated on ratings. In editorial rooms, publishing houses, and similar venues, a "rating mindset" reigns. Wherever you look, people are thinking in terms of market success. Only thirty years ago, and since the middle of the nineteenth century—since Baudelaire and Flaubert and others in avant-garde milieux of writers' writers, writers acknowledged by other writers or even artists acknowledged by other artists—immediate market success was suspect. It was taken as a sign of compromise with the times, with money . . . Today, on the contrary, the market is accepted more and more as a legitimate means of legitimation. You can see this in another recent institution, the best-seller list. Just this morning on the radio I heard an announcer, obviously very sure of himself, run through the latest best-seller list and decree that "philosophy is hot this year, since *Le Monde de Sophie* sold eight hundred thousand copies."[5] For him this verdict was absolute, like a final decree, provable by the number of copies sold. Audience ratings impose the sales model on cultural products. But it is important to know that, historically, all of the cultural productions that I consider (and I'm not alone here, at least I hope not) the highest human products—math, poetry, literature, philosophy—were all produced against market imperatives. It is very disturbing to see this ratings mindset established even among avant-garde publishers and intellectual institutions, both of which have begun to move into marketing, because it jeopardizes works that may not necessarily meet audience expectations but, in time, can create their own audience.

The phenomenon of audience ratings has a very particular effect on television. It appears in the pressure to get things out in a hurry. The competition among newspapers, like that between newspapers and television, shows up as competition for time—the pressure to get a scoop, to get there first. In a book of interviews with journalists, Alain Accardo shows how, simply because a competing network has "covered" a flood, television journalists have to "cover" the same flood and try to get something the other network missed. In short, stories are pushed on viewers because they are pushed on the producers; and they are pushed on producers by competition with other producers. This sort of cross pressure that journalists force on each other generates a whole series of consequences that translates into programming choices, into absences and presences.

At the beginning of this talk, I claimed that television is not very favorable to the expression of thought, and I set up a negative connection between time pressures and thought. It's an old philosophical topic—take the opposition that Plato makes between the philosopher, who has time, and people in the *agora*, in public space, who are in a hurry and under pressure. What he says, more or less, is that you can't think when you're in a hurry. It's a perspective that's clearly aristocratic, the viewpoint of a privileged person who has time and doesn't ask too many questions about the privileges that bestow this time. But this is not the place for that discussion. What is certain is the connection between thought and time. And one of the major problems posed by television is that question of the relationships between time and speed. Is it possible to think fast? By giving the floor to thinkers who are considered able to think at high speed, isn't television doomed to never have anything but *fast-thinkers*, thinkers who think faster than a speeding bullet . . . ?

In fact, what we have to ask is why these individuals are able to respond in these absolutely particular conditions, why and how they can think under these conditions in which nobody can think. The answer, it seems to me, is that they think in clichés, in the "received ideas" that Flaubert talks about—banal, conventional, common ideas that are received generally. By the time they reach you, these ideas have already been received by everybody else, so reception is never a problem. But whether you're talking about a speech, a book, or a message on television, the major question of communication is whether the conditions for reception have been fulfilled: Does the person who's listening have the tools to decode what I'm saying? When you transmit a "received idea," it's as if everything is set, and the problem solves itself. Communication is instantaneous because, in a sense, it has not occurred; or it only seems to have taken place. The exchange of commonplaces is communication with no content other than the fact of communication itself. The "commonplaces" that play such an enormous role in daily conversation work because everyone can ingest them immediately. Their very banality makes them something the speaker and the listener have in common. At the opposite end of the spectrum, thought, by definition, is subversive. It begins by taking apart "received ideas" and then presents the evidence in a demonstration, a logical proof. When Descartes talks about demonstration, he's talking about a logical chain of reasoning. Making an argument like this takes time, since you have to set out a series of propositions connected by "therefore," "consequently," "that said," "given the fact that . . ." Such a deployment of *thinking* thought, of thought in he process of being thought, is intrinsically dependent on time.

If television rewards a certain number of *fast-thinkers* who offer cultural "fast food"—predigested and prethought culture—it is not only because those who speak regularly on television are virtually on call (that, too, is tied to the sense of urgency in television news production). The list of commentators varies little (for Russia, call Mr. or Mrs. X, for Germany, it's Mr. Y). These "authorities" spare journalists the trouble of looking for people who really have something to say, in most cases younger, still-unknown people who are involved in their research and not much for talking to the media. These are the people who should be sought out. But the media mavens are always right on hand, set to churn out a paper or give an interview. And, of course, they are the special kind of thinkers who can "think" in these conditions where no one can do so.

DEBATES TRULY FALSE OR FALSELY TRUE

Now we must take on the question of televised debates. First of all, there are debates that are entirely bogus, and immediately recognizable as such. A television talk show with Alain Minc and Jacques Attali, or Alain Minc and Guy Sorman, or Luc Ferry and Alain Finkielkraut, or Jacques Julliard and Claude Imbert is a clear example, where you know the commentors are birds of a feather.[6] (In the U.S., some people earn their living just going from campus to campus in duets like these . . .) These people know each other, lunch together, have dinner together. Guillaume Durand once did a program about elites.[7] They were all on hand: Attali, Sarkozy, Minc . . . At one point, Attali was talking to Sarkozy and said, "Nicolas . . . Sarkozy," with a pause between the first and last name. If he'd stopped after the first name, it would've been obvious to the French viewer that they were cronies, whereas they are called on to represent opposite sides of the political fence. It was a tiny signal of complicity that could easily have gone unnoticed. In fact, the milieu of television regulars is a closed world that functions according to a model of permanent self-reinforcement. Here are people who are at odds but in an utterly conventional way; Julliard and Imbert, for example, are supposed to represent the Left and the Right. Referring to someone who twists words, the Kabyles say, *"he put my east in the west."* Well, these people put the Right on the Left. Is the public aware of this collusion? It's not certain. It can be seen in the wholesale rejection of Paris by people who live in the provinces (which the fascist criticism of Parisianism tries to appropriate). It came out a lot during the strikes last November: "All that is just Paris blowing off steam." People sense that something's going on, but they don't see how closed in on itself this milieu is, closed to their problems and, for that matter, to them.

There are also debates that seem genuine, but are falsely so. One quick example only, the debate organized by Cavada during those November strikes.[8] I've chosen this example because it looked for all the world like a democratic debate. This only makes my case all the stronger. (I shall proceed here as I have so far, moving from what's most obvious to what's most concealed.) When you look at what happened during this debate, you uncover a string of censorship.

First, there's the moderator. Viewers are always stuck by just how interventionist the moderator is. He determines the subject and decides the question up for debate (which often, as in Durand's debate over "should elites be burned?", turns out to be so absurd that the responses, whatever they are, are absurd as well). He keeps debaters in line with the rules of the game, even and especially because these rules can be so variable. They are different for a union organizer and for a member of the Academie Française. The moderator decides who speaks, and he hands out little tokens of prestige. Sociologists have examined the nonverbal components of verbal communication, how we say as much by our looks, our silences, our gestures, imitations and eye movements, and so on, as we do with our words. Intonation counts, as do all manner of other things. Much of what we reveal is beyond our conscious control (this ought to bother anyone who believes in the truth of Narcissus's mirror). There are so many registers of human expression,

even on the level of the words alone—if you keep pronunciation under control, then it's grammar that goes down the tubes,
and so on—that no one, not even the most self-controlled
individual, can master everything, unless obviously playing a
role or using terribly stilted language. The moderator intervenes with another language, one that he's not even aware of,
which can be perceived by listening to how the questions are
posed, and their tone. Some of the participants will get a curt
call to order, "Answer the question, please, you haven't answered my question," or "I'm waiting for your answer. Are
you going to stay out on strike or not?" Another telling example is all the different ways to say "thank you." "Thank
you" can mean "Thank you ever so much, I am really in your
debt, I am awfully happy to have your thoughts on this issue";
then there's the "thank you" that amounts to a dismissal, an
effective "OK, that's enough of that. Who's next?" All of this
comes out in tiny ways, in infinitesimal nuances of tone, but
the discussants are affected by it all, the hidden semantics no
less than the surface syntax.

The moderator also allots time and sets the tone, respectful
or disdainful, attentive or impatient. For example, a preemptory "yeah, yeah, yeah" alerts the discussant to the moderator's impatience or lack of interest . . . In the interviews that
my research team conducts it has become clear that it is very
important to signal our agreement and interest; otherwise the
interviewees get discouraged and gradually stop talking.
They're waiting for little signs—a "yes, that's right," a nod
that they've been heard and understood. These imperceptible
signs are manipulated by him, more often unconsciously than
consciously. For example, an exaggerated respect for high culture can lead the moderator, as a largely self-taught person
with a smattering of high culture, to admire false great personages, academicians and people with titles that compel respect. Moderators can also manipulate pressure and urgency.
They can use the clock to cut someone off, to push, to interrupt. Here, they have yet another resource. All moderators

turn themselves into representatives of the public at large: "I have to interrupt you here, I don't understand what you mean." What comes across is not that the moderator is dumb—no moderator will let that happen—but that the average viewer (dumb by definition) won't understand. The moderator appears to be interrupting an intelligent speech to speak for the "dummies." In fact, as I have been able to see for myself, it's the people in whose name the moderator is supposedly acting who are the most exasperated by such interference.

The result is that, all in all, during a two-hour program, the union delegate had exactly five minutes to speak (even though everybody knows that if the union hadn't been involved, there wouldn't have been any strike, and no program either, and so on). Yet, on the surface—and this is why Cavada's program is significant—the program adhered to all the formal signs of equality.

This poses a very serious problem for democratic practice. Obviously, all discussants in the studio are not equal. You have people who are both professional talkers and television pros, and, facing them, you have the rank amateurs (the strikers might know how to talk on their home turf but. . . .). The inequality is patent. To reestablish some equality, the moderator would have to be inegalitarian, by helping those clearly struggling in an unfamiliar situation—much as we did in the interviews for *La Misère du monde*. When you want someone who is not a professional talker of some sort to say something (and often these people say really quite extraordinary things that individuals who are constantly called upon to speak couldn't even imagine), you have to help people talk. To put it in nobler terms, I'll say that this is the Socratic mission in all its glory. You put yourself at the service of someone with something important to say, someone whose words you want to hear and whose thoughts interest you, and you work to help get the words out. But this isn't at all what television moderators do: not only do they not help people unaccustomed to public platforms but they inhibit them in many ways—by not ceding the floor at the right moment, by putting people on the spot unexpectedly, by showing impatience, and so on. .

But these are still things that are up-front and visible. We must look to the second level, to the way the group appearing on a given talk show is chosen. Because these choices determine what happens and how. And they are not arrived at on screen. There is a back-stage process of shaping the group that ends up in the studio for the show, beginning with the preliminary decisions about who gets invited and who doesn't. There are people whom no one would ever think of inviting, and others who are invited but decline. The set is there in front of viewers, and what they see hides what they don't see—and what they don't see, in this constructed image, are the social conditions of its construction. So no one ever says, "hey, so-and-so isn't there." Another example of this manipulation (one of a thousand possible examples): during the strikes, the *Cercle de minuit* talk show had two successive programs on intellectuals and the strikes. Overall, the intellectuals were divided into two main camps. During the first program, the intellectuals against the strikes appeared on the right side of the set. For the second, follow-up program the setup had been changed. More people were added on the right, and those in favor of the strikes were dropped. The people who appeared on the right during the first program appeared on the left during the second. Right and left are relative, by definition, so in this case, changing the arrangement on the set changed the message sent by the program.

The arrangement of the set is important because it is supposed to give the image of a democratic equilibrium. Equality is ostentatiously exaggerated, and the moderator comes across as the referee. The set for the Cavada program discussed earlier had two categories of people. On the one hand, there were the strikers themselves; and then there were others, also protagonists but cast in the position of observers. The first group was there to *explain themselves* ("Why are you doing this? Why are you upsetting everybody?" and so on), and the others were there to *explain things,* to make a metadiscourse, a talk about talk.

Another invisible yet absolutely decisive factor concerns the arrangements agreed upon with the participants prior to the show. This groundwork can create a sort of screenplay, more or less detailed, that the guests are obliged to follow. In certain cases, just as in certain games, preparation can almost turn into a rehearsal. This prescripted scenario leaves little room for improvisation, no room for an offhand, spontaneous word. This would be altogether too risky, even dangerous, both for the moderator and the program.

The model of what Ludwig Wittgenstein calls the language game is also useful here. The game about to be played has tacit rules, since television shows, like every social milieu in which discourse circulates, allow certain things to be said and proscribe others. The first, implicit assumption of this language game is rooted in the conception of democratic debates modeled on wrestling. There must be conflicts, with good guys and bad guys . . . Yet, at the same time, not all holds are allowed: the blows have to be clothed by the model of formal, intellectual language. Another feature of this space is the complicity between professionals that I mentioned earlier. The people I call "fast-thinkers," specialists in throw-away thinking—are known in the industry as "good guests." They're the people whom you can always invite because you know they'll be good company and won't create problems. They won't be difficult and they're smooth talkers. There is a whole world of "good guests" who take to the television format like fish to water— and then there are others who are like fish on dry land.

The final invisible element in play is the moderator's unconscious. It has often happened to me, even with journalists who are pretty much on my side, that I have to begin all my answers by going back over the question. Journalists, with their special "glasses" and their peculiar categories of thought, often ask questions that don't have anything to do with the matter at hand. For example, on the so-called "inner city problem," their heads are full of all the phantasms I mentioned earlier. So, before you can even begin to respond, you have to say, very politely, "Your question is certainly interesting, but it seems to me that there is another one that is even more important . . ." Otherwise, you end up answering questions that shouldn't be even asked.

CONTRADICTIONS AND TENSIONS

Television is an instrument of communication with very little autonomy, subject as it is to a whole series of pressures arising from the characteristic social relations between journalists. These include *relations of competition* (relentless and pitiless, even to the point of absurdity) and *relations of collusion*, derived from objective common interests. These interests in turn are a function of the journalists' position in the field of symbolic production and their shared cognitive, perceptual, and evaluative structures, which they share by virtue of common social background and training (or lack thereof). It follows that this instrument of communication, as much as it appears to run free, is in fact reined in. During the 1960s, when television appeared on the cultural scene as a new phenomenon,[9] a certain number of "sociologists" (quotation marks needed here) rushed to proclaim that, as a "means of mass communication," television was going to "massify" everything. It was going to be the great leveler and turn all viewers into one big, undifferentiated mass. In fact, this assessment seriously underestimated viewers' capacity for resistance. But, above all, it underestimated television's ability to transform its very producers and the other journalists that compete with it and, ultimately, through its irresistible fascination for some of them, the ensemble of cultural producers. The most important development, and a difficult one to foresee, was the extraordinary extension of the power of television over the whole of cultural production, including scientific and artistic production.

Today, television has carried to the extreme, to the very

limit, a contradiction that haunts every sphere of cultural production. I am referring to the contradiction between the economic and social conditions necessary to produce a certain
type of work and the social conditions of transmission for the
products obtained under these conditions. I used math as an
obvious example, but my argument also holds for avant-garde
poetry, philosophy, sociology, and so on, works thought to be
"pure" (a ridiculous word in any case), but which are, let's say,
at least relatively independent of the market. There is a basic,
fundamental contradiction between the conditions that allow
one to do cutting-edge math or avant-garde poetry, and so on,
and the conditions necessary to transmit these things to everybody else. Television carries this contradiction to the extreme
to the extent that, through audience ratings and more than all
the other milieux of cultural production, it is subject to market
pressures.

By the same token, in this microcosm that is the world of
journalism, tension is very high between those who would like
to defend the values of independence, freedom from market
demands, freedom from made-to-order programs, and from
managers, and so on, and those who submit to this necessity
and are rewarded accordingly . . .Given the strength of the
opposition, these tensions can hardly be expressed, at least not
on screen. I am thinking here of the opposition between the big
stars with big salaries who are especially visible and especially
rewarded, but who are also especially subject to all these pressures, and the invisible drones who put the news together, do
the reporting, and who are becoming more and more critical of
the system. Increasingly well-trained in the logic of the job
market, they are assigned to jobs that are more and more
pedestrian, more and more insignificant—behind the micro-
phones and the cameras you have people who are incomparably more cultivated than their counterparts in the 1960's. In
other words, this tension between what the profession requires
and the aspirations that people acquire in journalism school or
in college is greater and greater—even though there is also

anticipatory socialization on the part of people really on the make . . . One journalist said recently that the midlife crisis at forty (which is when you used to find out that your job isn't everything you thought it would be) has moved back to thirty. People are discovering earlier the terrible requirements of this work and in particular, all the pressures associated with audience ratings and other such gauges. Journalism is one of the areas where you find the greatest number of people who are anxious, dissatisfied, rebellious, or cynically resigned, where very often (especially, obviously, for those on the bottom rung of the ladder) you find anger, revulsion, or discouragement about work that is experienced as or proclaimed to be "not like other jobs." But we're far from a situation where this spite or these refusals could take the form of true resistance, and even farther from the possibility of collective resistance.

To understand all this—especially all the phenomena that, in spite of all my efforts, it might be thought I was blaming on the moderators as individuals—we must move to the level of global mechanisms, to the structural level. Plato (I am citing him a lot today) said that we are god's puppets. Television is a universe where you get the impression that social actors—even when they seem to be important, free, and independent, and even sometimes possessed of an extraordinary aura (just take a look at the television magazines)—are the puppets of a necessity that we must understand, of a structure that we must unearth and bring to light.

PART TWO

Invisible Structures and Their Effects

To move beyond a description, however meticulous, of what happens in a television studio, in order to try and grasp the explanatory mechanisms of journalistic practice, I have to introduce a somewhat technical term—the idea of the journalistic field. Journalism is a microcosm with its own laws, defined both by its position in the world at large and by the attractions and repulsions to which it is subject from other such microcosms. To say that it is independent or autonomous, that it has its own laws, is to say that what happens in it cannot be understood by looking only at external factors. That is why I did not want to explain what happens in journalism as a function of economic factors. What happens on TF1 cannot be explained simply by the fact that it is owned by the Bouygues holding company. Any explanation that didn't take this fact into account would obviously be inadequate, but an explanation based solely on it would be just as inadequate—more inadequate still, perhaps, precisely because it would seem adequate. This half-baked version of materialism, associated with Marxism, condemns without shedding light anywhere and ultimately explains nothing.

MARKETSHARE AND COMPETITION

To understand what goes on at TF1, you have to take into account everything that TF1 owes to its location in a universe of objective relations between the different, competing television networks. You also have to recognize that the form this competition takes is defined invisibly by unperceived power relations that can be grasped through indicators like market-share, the weight given to advertising, the collective capital of high-status journalists, and so on. In other words, not only are there interactions between these news media—between people who do or do not speak to each other, people who influence each other and read each other's work, everything on which I've touched up to now—there are also completely invisible power relations. These invisible relations mean that, in order to understand what goes on at TF1 or Arte, you have to take into account the totality of the objective power relations that structure the field. In the field of economic enterprises, for example, a very powerful company has the power to alter virtually the entire economic playing field. By lowering its prices and setting up a sort of entry barrier, it can forestall the entry into the market of new enterprises. These effects are not necessarily deliberate or intended. TF1 transformed television simply by accumulating a set of specific powers that influence this universe and are translated into an increased share of the market. Neither the viewers nor the journalists are able to see this structure. Journalists see its effects, but they don't see the extent to which the relative weight of the institution for which they work weighs on them, on their place within it and their own ability to affect this same institution. To try and understand what journalists are able to do, you have to keep in mind a series of parameters: first, the relative position of the particular news medium, whether it's TF1 or *Le Monde*; and second, the positions occupied by journalists themselves within the space occupied by their respective newspapers or networks.

A field is a structured social space, a field of forces, a force field. It contains people who dominate and others who are dominated. Constant, permanent relationships of inequality operate inside this space, which at the same time becomes a space in which the various actors struggle for the transformation or preservation of the field. All the individuals in this universe bring to the competition all the (relative) power at their disposal. It is this power that defines their position in the field and, as a result, their strategies. Economic competition between networks or newspapers for viewers, readers, or for marketshare, takes place concretely in the form of a contest between journalists. This contest has its own, specific stakes — the scoop, the "exclusive," professional reputations, and so on. This kind of competition is neither experienced nor thought of as a struggle purely for economic gain, even though it remains subject to pressures deriving from the position the news medium itself occupies within a larger set of economic and symbolic power relations. Today, invisible but objective relations connect people and parties who may never meet — say, the very serious monthly *Le Monde diplomatique*, at one extreme, and the TF1 television channel, at the other. Nevertheless, in everything these entities do, they are led, consciously or unconsciously, to take into account the same pressures and effects, because they belong to the same world. In other words, if I want to find out what one or another journalist is going to say or write, or will find obvious or unthinkable, normal or worthless, I have to know the position that journalist occupies in this space. I need to know, as well, the specific power of the news medium in question. This impact can be measured by indicators such as the economic weight it pulls, that is, its share of the market. But its symbolic weight also comes into play, and that is much more difficult to quantify. (In fact, to be complete, the position of the national media field within the global media field would have to be taken into account. We'd also have to bring in the economic-technical, and especially, the symbolic dominance of American television, which serves a good many journalists as both a model and a source of ideas, formulas, and tactics.)

To understand this structure better in its current form, it's a good idea to go back over how it was established. During the 1950s, in France, television was barely a factor in the journalistic field. Hardly anyone thought about TV. Television workers were doubly dominated: culturally and symbolically, in terms of prestige, because they were suspected of being depen-

dent on the political powers-that-be; and economically, because they were dependent on government subsidies and
therefore much less efficient and much less powerful than their
autonomous private counterparts. With time (the process war-
rants detailed examination) this relationship was completely
reversed, so that television now dominates the journalistic field
both economically and symbolically. The general crisis faced
by newspapers today makes this domination particularly con-
spicuous. Some newspapers are simply folding, and others are
forced to spend every minute worrying about their very sur-
vival, about getting their audience, or getting it back. The most
threatened, at least in France, are the papers that used to spe-
cialize in human interest stories or sports: they simply don't
have much to offer against television programming that focuses more and more on sports and human interest stories,
circumventing the rules set by serious journalism (which puts,
or used to put, on the front-page foreign affairs, politics, even
political analysis, giving lesser placement to human interest
stories and sports).

Of course, this description is a rough one. It would be necessary to go into much more detail to provide a social history
of the evolving relationships between the different media (as
opposed to histories of a single newspaper or other news
medium)—something that unfortunately doesn't exist. It's on
this level of structural history that the most important things
appear. What counts in a field is relative weight, relative impact. A newspaper can remain absolutely the same, not lose a
single reader, and yet be profoundly altered because its relative
importance in the field has changed. For example, a newspaper
ceases to dominate the field when it loses the power to lay
down the law. It can certainly be said that Le Monde used to
lay down the law in France in the world of print journalism. A
field already existed, divided between the poles recognized by
all historians of journalism, consisting of newspapers that give
news—stories and events—and newspapers that give views—
opinions and analysis; between mass circulation newspapers

such as *France Soir* and newspapers with relatively small circulation that are nonetheless endowed with a semiofficial authority. *Le Monde* was in a good position on both counts: it had a large enough circulation to draw advertisers, and it had enough symbolic capital to be an authority. It held both factors of power in the field simultaneously.

Such "newspapers of opinion and analysis" appeared in France at the end of the nineteenth century as a reaction to the mass circulation sensational press. Educated readers have always viewed the sensational papers with fear or distrust or both. Television—the mass medium par excellence—is therefore unprecedented only in its scope. Here I'll make an aside. One of the great problems faced by sociologists is how to avoid falling into one or the other of two symmetrical illusions. On the one hand, there is the sense of something that has never been seen before. (There are sociologists who love this business, and it's very much the thing, especially on television, to announce the appearance of incredible phenomena or revolutions.) And, on the other hand (mostly from conservative sociologists), there's the opposite, "the way it always has been," "there's nothing new under the sun," "there'll always be people on top and people on the bottom," "the poor are always with us; and the rich too . . ." The already-great risk of falling into such traps is all the greater because historical comparison is extremely difficult. Comparisons can only be made from structure to structure, and there is always the chance that you will make a mistake and describe as extraordinary something that is totally banal, simply because you don't know any better. This is one of the things that can make journalists dangerous. Since they're not always very educated, they marvel at things that aren't very marvelous and don't marvel at things that are in fact extraordinary . . . History is indispensable to sociologists. Unfortunately, in a good many areas, especially for the history of the present, the available studies are inadequate. This is particularly true in the case of new phenomena, such as journalism.

MAKING EVERYTHING ORDINARY

To return to the problem of television's effects, it is true that the opposition between news and analysis existed before, but never with this intensity. (You see here that I'm steering between "never-been-seen-before" and "the-way-it-always-has-been.") Television's power of diffusion means that it poses a terrible problem for the print media and for culture generally. Next to it, the mass circulation press that sent so many shudders up educated spines in earlier times doesn't seem like much at all. (Raymond Williams argued that the entire romantic revolution in poetry was brought about by the horror that English writers felt at the beginnings of the mass circulation press.[10]) By virtue of its reach and exceptional power, television produces effects which, though not without precedent, are completely original.

For example, the evening news on French TV brings together more people than all the French newspapers together, morning and evening editions included. When the information supplied by a single news medium becomes a universal source of news, the resulting political and cultural effects are clear. Everybody knows the "law" that if a newspaper or other news vehicle wants to reach a broad public, it has to dispense with sharp edges and anything that might divide or exclude readers (just think about *Paris-Match* or, in the U.S., *Life* magazine). It must attempt to be inoffensive, not to "offend anyone," and it must never bring up problems—or, if it does, only problems that don't pose any problem. People talk so much about the weather in day-to-day life because it's a subject that cannot cause trouble. Unless you're on vacation and talking with a farmer who needs rain, the weather is the absolutely ideal *soft* subject. The farther a paper extends its circulation, the more it favors such topics that interest "everybody" and don't raise problems. The object—news—is constructed in accordance with the perceptual categories of the receiver.

The collective activity I've described works so well precisely because of this homogenization, which smoothes over things, brings them into line, and depoliticizes them. And it works even though, strictly speaking, this activity is without a subject, that is, no one ever thought of or wished for it as such. This is something that is observed frequently in social life. Things happen that nobody wants but seem somehow to have been willed. Herein lies the danger of simplistic criticism. It takes the place of the work necessary to understand phenomena such as the fact that, even though no one really wished it this way, and without any intervention on the part of the people actually paying for it, we end up with this very strange product, the "TV news." It suits everybody because it confirms what they already know and, above all, leaves their mental structures intact. There are revolutions, the ones we usually talk about, that aim at the material bases of a society—take the nationalization of Church property after 1789—and then there are symbolic revolutions effected by artists, scholars, or great religious or (sometimes, though less often) political prophets. These affect our mental structures, which means that they change the ways we see and think. Manet is an example: his painting upset the fundamental structure of all academic teaching of painting in the nineteenth century, the opposition between the contemporary and the traditional.[11] If a vehicle as powerful as television were oriented even slightly toward this kind of symbolic revolution, I can assure you that everyone would be rushing to put a stop to it . . .

But it turns out that, without anyone having to ask television to work this way, the model of competition and the mechanisms outlined above ensure that television does nothing of the sort. It is perfectly adapted to the mental structures of its audience. I could point to television's moralizing, telethon side, which needs to be analyzed from this perspective. André Gide used to say that worthy sentiments make bad literature. But worthy sentiments certainly make for good audience ratings. The moralizing bent of television should make us wonder how cynical individuals are able to make such astoundingly conservative, moralizing statements. Our news anchors, our talk show hosts, and our sports announcers have turned into two-bit spiritual guides, representatives of middle-class morality. They are always telling us what we "should think" about what they call "social problems," such as violence in the inner city or in the schools. The same is true for art and literature, where the best-known of the so-called literary programs serve the establishment and ever-more obsequiously promote social conformity and market values.[12]

Journalists—we should really say the journalistic field—owe their importance in society to their de facto monopoly on the large-scale informational instruments of production and diffusion of information. Through these, they control the access of ordinary citizens but also of other cultural producers such as scholars, artists, and writers, to what is sometimes called "public space," that is, the space of mass circulation. (This is the monopoly that blocks the way whenever an individual or member of a group tries to get a given piece of news into broad circulation.) Even though they occupy an inferior, dominated position in the fields of cultural production, journalists exercise a very particular form of domination, since they control the means of public expression. They control, in effect, public existence, one's ability to be recognized as a *public figure,* obviously critical for politicians and certain intellectuals. This position means that at least the most important of these figures are treated with a respect that is often quite out of proportion with their intellectual merits . . . Moreover, they are able to use part of this power of consecration to their own benefit. Even the best-known journalists occupy positions of structural inferiority vis-à-vis social categories such as intellectuals or politicians—and journalists want nothing so much as to be part of the intellectual crowd. No doubt, this structural inferiority goes a long way to explain their tendency toward anti-intellectualism. Nevertheless, they are able to dominate members of these "superior" categories on occasion.

Above all, though, with their permanent access to public visibility, broad circulation, and mass diffusion—an access that was completely unthinkable for any cultural producer until television came into the picture—these journalists can impose on the whole of society their vision of the world, their conception of problems, and their point of view. The objection can be raised that the world of journalism is divided, differentiated, and diversified, and as such can very well represent all opinions and points of view or let them be expressed. (It is true that to break through journalism's protective shield, you can to a certain extent and provided you possess a minimum of symbolic capital on your own, play journalists and media off against one another.) Yet it remains true that, like other fields, the journalistic field is based on a set of shared assumptions and beliefs, which reach beyond differences of position and opinion. These assumptions operate within a particular set of mental categories; they reside in a characteristic relationship to language, and are visible in everything implied by a formulation such as "it's just *made* for television." These are what supplies the principle that determines what journalists select both within social reality and among symbolic productions as a whole. There is no discourse (scientific analysis, political manifesto, whatever) and no action (demonstration, strike) that doesn't have to face this trial of journalistic selection in order to catch the public eye. The effect is *censorship*, which journalists practice without even being aware of it. They retain only the things capable of *interesting* them and "keeping their attention," which means things that fit their categories and mental grid; and they reject as insignificant or remain indifferent to symbolic expressions that ought to reach the population as a whole.

Another consequence, one more difficult to grasp, of television's increased (relative) power in the space of the means of diffusion and of the greater market pressures on this newly dominant medium, shows up in the shift from a national cultural policy, which once worked through television, to a sort of spontaneistic demagoguery. While this change affects television in particular, it has also contaminated supposedly serious newspapers—witness the greater and greater space given over to letters to the editor and op-ed pieces. In the 1950s, television in France was openly "cultural": it used its monopoly to influence virtually every product that laid claim to high cultural status (documentaries, adaptations of the classics, cultural debates, and so forth) and to raise the taste of the general public. In the 1990s, because it must reach the largest audience possible, television is intent on exploiting and pandering to these same tastes. It does so by offering viewers what are essentially raw products, of which the paradigmatic program is the talk show with its "slices of life." These lived experiences come across as unbuttoned exhibitions of often extreme behavior aimed at satisfying a kind of voyeurism and exhibitionism. (TV game shows, which people are dying to get on, if only as a member of the studio audience, just to have a moment of visibility, are another example.) That said, I don't share the nostalgia professed by some people for the paternalistic-pedagogical television of the past, which I see as no less opposed to a truly democratic use of the means of mass circulation than populist spontaneism and demagogic capitulation to popular tastes.

STRUGGLES SETTLED BY AUDIENCE RATINGS

So you have to look beyond appearances, beyond what happens in the studio, and even beyond the competition inside the journalistic field. To the extent that it decides the very form of onscreen interactions, one must understand the power relationship between the different news media. To understand why we continually see the same debates between the same journalists, we have to consider the position of the various media that these journalists represent and their position within those media. Similarly, both of these factors have to be kept in mind if we want to understand what a reporter for *Le Monde* can and cannot write. What are actually positional pressures are experienced as ethical interdictions or injunctions: "that's not the practice at *Le Monde*" or "that doesn't fit with *Le Monde*'s culture," or again, "that just isn't done here," and so on. All these experiences, presented as ethical precepts, translate the structure of the field through an individual who occupies a particular position in this space.

Competitors within a given field often have polemical images of one another. They produce stereotypes about one another and insults as well. (In the world of sports, for example, rugby players routinely refer to soccer players as "armless wonders.") These images are often strategies that take into account and make use of power relationships, which they aim to transform or preserve. These days, print journalists, in particular those who occupy a dominated position within this sphere (that is, those who write for lesser newspapers and are in lesser positions) are elaborating a discourse that is highly critical of television.

In fact, these images themselves take a stand, which essentially gives expression to the position occupied by the individual who, with greater or lesser disclaimers, articulates the view in question. At the same time, these strategies aim to transform the position this individual occupies in the field. Today, the struggle over television is central to the journalistic milieu, and its centrality makes it very difficult to study. Much pseudo-scholarly discourse on television does no more than record what TV people say about TV. (Journalists are all the more inclined to say that a sociologist is good when what he says is close to what they think. Which means—and it's probably a good thing, too—that you haven't a prayer of being popular with TV people if you try to tell the truth about television.) That said, there are indicators that, relative to television, print journalism is in gradual retreat. Witness the increasing space given to TV listings in newspapers, or the great store set by journalists in having their stories picked up by television, as well as, obviously, being seen on television. Such visibility gives them greater status in their newspaper or journal. Any journalist who wants power or influence has to have a TV program. It is even possible for television journalists to get important positions in the printed press. This calls into question the specificity of writing, and, for that matter, the specificity of the entire profession. The fact that a television news anchor can become the editor of a newspaper or news magazine from one day to the next makes you wonder just what the specific competence required of a journalist might be.

Then there is the fact that television more and more defines what Americans call the *agenda* (the issues up for discussion, the subjects of the editorials, important problems to be covered). In the circular circulation of information I've described, television carries decisive weight. If the printed press should happen to raise an issue—a scandal or a debate—it becomes central only when television takes it up and gives it full orchestration, and, thereby, political impact. This dependence on television threatens the position of print journalists, and this too calls the specificity of the profession into question. Of course, all of this needs to be documented and verified. What I'm giving here is simultaneously a balance sheet based on a number of studies and a program for further research. These are very complicated matters about which knowledge cannot really advance without significant empirical work. This doesn't prevent the practitioners of "mediology," self-designated specialists in a science that doesn't exist, from drawing all sorts of peremptory conclusions about the state of media in the world today before any study has been conducted.

But the most important point is that through the increased symbolic power of television overall, and, among the competing kinds of television, the increased influence of the most cynical and most successful seekers after anything sensational, spectacular, or extraordinary, a certain vision of the news comes to take over the whole of the journalistic field. Until recently, this conception of the news had been relegated to the tabloids specializing in sports and human interest stories. Similarly, a certain category of journalists, recruited at great cost for their ability immediately to fulfill the expectations of the public that expects the least—journalists who are necessarily the most cynical, the most indifferent to any kind of structural analysis, and even more reluctant to engage in any inquiry that touches on politics—tends to impose on all journalists its "values," its preferences, its ways of being and speaking, its "human ideal." Pushed by competition for marketshare, television networks have greater and greater recourse to the tried and true formulas of tabloid journalism, with emphasis (when not the entire newscast) devoted to human interest stories or sports. No matter what has happened in the world on a given day, more and more often the evening news begins with French soccer scores or another sporting event, interrupting the regular news. Or it will highlight the most anecdotal, ritualized political event (visits of foreign heads of state, the president's trips abroad, and so on), or the natural disasters, accidents, fires and the like. In short, the focus is on those things which are apt to arouse curiosity but require no analysis, especially in the political sphere.

As I've said, human interest stories create a political vacuum. They depoliticize and reduce what goes on in the world to the level of anecdote or scandal. This can occur on a national or international scale, especially with film stars or members of royal families, and is accomplished by fixing and keeping attention fixed on events without political consequences, but which are nonetheless dramatized so as to "draw a lesson" or be transformed into illustrations of "social problems." This is where our TV philosophers are called in to give meaning to the meaningless, anecdotal, or fortuitous event that has been artificially brought to stage center and given significance—a headscarf worn to school, an assault on a schoolteacher or any other "social fact" tailor-made to arouse the pathos and indignation of some commentators or the tedious moralizing of others. This same search for sensational news, and hence market success, can also lead to the selection of stories that give free rein to the unbridled constructions of demagoguery (whether spontaneous or intentional) or can stir up great excitement by catering to the most primitive drives and emotions (with stories of kidnapped children and scandals likely to arouse public indignation). Purely sentimental and therapeutic forms of mobilizing feelings can come into play, but, with murders of children or incidents tied to stigmatized groups, other forms of mobilization can also take place, forms that are just as emotional but aggressive enough almost to qualify as symbolic lynching.

It follows that the printed press today faces a choice: Should it go in the direction of the dominant model, which means publishing newspapers that resemble TV news, or should it emphasize its difference and engage instead in a strategy of product differentiation? Should it compete, and run the risk of losing on both fronts, not reaching a mass public while losing the one that remains faithful to the strict definition of the cultural message? Or, once again, should it stress its difference? The same problem exists inside the television field itself, which is, of course, a subfield within the larger journalistic field. From my observations so far, I think that, unconsciously, those in charge, who are themselves victims of the "audience ratings mindset," don't really choose. (It is regularly observed that major social decisions aren't made by anyone. If sociologists always disturb things, it's because they force us to make conscious things that we'd rather leave unconscious.) I think that the general trend is for old-style means of cultural production to lose their specificity and move onto a terrain where they can't win. Thus, the cultural network Channel 7 (now Arte) moved from a policy of intransigent, even aggressive, esotericism to a more or less disreputable compromise with audience ratings. The result is programming that makes concessions to facile, popular programming during prime time and keeps the esoteric fare for late at night. *Le Monde* (like other serious newspapers throughout the world) currently faces the same choice. I think I've said enough to show the move from the analysis of invisible structures—a bit like the force of gravity, things that nobody sees but have to be accepted for us to understand what's going on—to individual experience, and how the invisible power relations are translated into personal conflicts and existential choices.

The journalistic field has one distinguishing characteristic: it is much more dependent on external forces than the other fields of cultural production, such as mathematics, literature, law, science, and so on. It depends very directly on demand, since, and perhaps even more than the political field itself, it is subject to the decrees of the market and the opinion poll. The conflict of "pure" versus "market" can be seen in every field. In the theater, for example, it turns up in the opposition between big, popular shows and avant-garde theater, between Broadway musicals and off-Broadway experimental theater. In the media, it's the difference between TF1 and *Le Monde*. All reflect the same opposition between catering to a public that is more educated, on the one hand, less so on the other, with more students for the one, more businessmen for the other. But if this opposition is ubiquitous, it's particularly brutal in the journalistic field, where the market weighs particularly heavily. Its intensity is unprecedented and currently without equal. Furthermore, the journalistic field has no equivalent of the sort of immanent justice in the scientific world that censures those individuals who break certain rules and rewards those who abide by them with the esteem of their peers (as manifested most notably in citations and references). Where are the positive or negative sanctions for journalism? The only criticism consists of satirical spoofs such as that on the Puppets.[13] As for the rewards, there is little more than the possibility of having one's story "picked up" (copied by another journalist), but this indicator is infrequent, not very visible, and ambiguous.

THE POWER OF TELEVISION

The world of journalism in itself is a field, but one that is subject to great pressure from the economic field via audience ratings. This very heteronomous field, which is structurally very strongly subordinated to market pressures, in turn applies pressure to all other fields. This structural, objective, anonymous and invisible effect has nothing to do with what is visible or with what television usually gets attacked for, namely, the direct intervention of one or another individual . . . It is not enough, it should not be enough, to attack the people in charge. For example, Karl Kraus, the great Viennese satirist early in this century, launched violent attacks on a man who was the equivalent of the editor of *Le Nouvel Observateur*. He denounced the cultural conformism so destructive of culture and the complacency of minor or measly writers whom he saw as discrediting pacifist ideas by championing them hypocritically . . . As a general rule, critics are concerned with individuals. But when you do sociology, you learn that men and women are indeed responsible, but that what they can or cannot do is largely determined by the structure in which they are placed and by the positions they occupy within that structure. So polemical attacks on this or that journalist, philosopher, or philosopher-journalist are not enough . . . Everyone has a favorite whipping boy, and I'm no exception. Bernard-Henri Lévy has become something of a symbol of the writer-journalist and the philosopher-journalist. But no sociologist worthy of the name talks about Bernard-Henri Lévy.[14] It is vital to understand that he is only a sort of structural epiphenomenon, and that, like an electron, he is the expression of a field. You can't understand anything if you don't understand the field that produces him and gives him his parcel of power.

This understanding is important both to remove the analysis from the level of drama and to direct action rationally. I am in fact convinced (and this presentation on television bears witness to this conviction) that analyses like this can perhaps help to change things. Every science makes this claim. Auguste Comte, the founder of sociology, proclaimed that "science leads to foresight, and foresight leads to action." Social science has as much right to this aspiration as any other science. By describing a space such as journalism, investing it from the beginning with drives, feelings, and emotions—emotions and drives that are glossed over by the work of analysis—sociologists can hope to have some effect. Increasing awareness of the mechanisms at work, for example, can help by offering a measure of freedom to those manipulated by these mechanisms, whether they are journalists or viewers. Another aside: I think (or at least I hope) that if they really listen to what I am saying, journalists who might initially feel attacked will feel that, by spelling out things they know vaguely but don't really want to know too much about, I am giving them instruments of freedom with which to master the mechanisms I discuss.

In fact, it might be possible to create alliances between news media that could cancel out certain of the structural effects of competition that are most pernicious, such as the race for the scoop. Some of these dangerous effects derive from the structural effects shaping the competition, which produces a sense of urgency and leads to the race for the scoop. This means that news which might prove dangerous to those involved can be broadcast simply to beat out a competitor, with no thought given to the danger. To the extent that this is true, making these mechanisms conscious or explicit could lead to an arrangement that would neutralize competition. In a scenario somewhat like what sometimes happens now in extreme cases, as when children are kidnapped, for example, one could imagine—or dream—that journalists might agree to forget about audience ratings for once and refuse to open their talk shows to political leaders known for and by their xenophobia. Further, they could agree not to broadcast what these characters say. (This would be infinitely more effective than all the so-called refutations put together.)

All of this is utopian, and I know it. But to those who always tax the sociologist with determinism and pessimism, I will only say that if people became aware of them, conscious action aimed at controlling the structural mechanisms that engender moral failure would be possible. As we have seen, this world characterized by a high degree of cynicism has a lot of talk about morality. As a sociologist, I know that morality only works if it is supported by structures and mechanisms that give people an interest in morality. And, for something like a moral anxiety to occur, that morality has to find support, reinforcement, and rewards in this structure. These rewards could also come from a public more enlightened and more aware of the manipulations to which it is subject.

I think that all the fields of cultural production today are subject to structural pressure from the journalistic field, and not from any one journalist or network executive, who are themselves subject to control by the field. This pressure exercises equivalent and systematic effects in every field. In other words, this journalistic field, which is more and more dominated by the market model, imposes its pressures more and more on other fields. Through pressure from audience ratings, economic forces weigh on television, and through its effect on journalism, television weighs on newspapers and magazines, even the "purest" among them. The weight then falls on individual journalists, who little by little let themselves be drawn into television's orbit. In this way, through the weight exerted by the journalistic field, the economy weighs on all fields of cultural production.

In a very interesting paper in a special issue on journalism of *Actes de la recherche en sciences sociales*, Remi Lenoir shows how, in the juridical world, a certain number of hard-hitting judges—not always the most respectable according to the norms internal to the juridical field—made use of television to change the power relations inside their field: essentially, they short-circuited internal hierarchies. This might be fine in some cases, but it can also endanger a stage of collective rationality that is achieved only with difficulty. Or, more precisely, it calls into question everything that has been acquired and guaranteed by the autonomy of a juridical world able to set its model of rationality against intuitive senses of justice and juridical common sense, both of which often give in to appearances or emotion. Whether expressing their vision and their own values or claiming, in all good faith, to represent "popular feeling," journalists can influence judges, sometimes very directly. This has led to talk of a veritable transfer of the power to judge. An equivalent could also be found in science, where, as shown in the "scandals" analyzed by Patrick Champagne, the demagogic model—precisely the model of audience ratings—takes precedence over that of internal criticism.[15]

All this may appear quite abstract. In each field, the university, history, whatever, there are those who dominate and those who are dominated according to the values internal to that field. A "good historian" is someone good historians call a good historian. The whole business is circular by definition. But heteronomy—the loss of autonomy through subjection to external forces—begins when someone who is not a mathematician intervenes to give an opinion about mathematics, or when someone who is not recognized as a historian (a historian who talks about history on television, for instance) gives an opinion about historians—and is listened to. With the "authority" conferred by television, Mr. Cavada tells you that Mr. X is the greatest French philosopher. Can you imagine a referendum or a debate between two parties chosen by a talk show host like Cavada settling an argument between two mathematicians, two biologists, or two physicists? But the media never fail to offer their verdicts. The weekly magazines love this sort of thing—summing up the decade, giving the hit parade of the "in" "intellectuals" of the year, the month, the week—the intellectuals who count, the ones on their way up or on their way down . . .

Why does this tactic meet with such success? Because these instruments let you play the intellectual stock market. They are used by intellectuals—who are the shareholders in this enterprise (often small shareholders to be sure, but powerful in journalism or publishing)—to increase the value of their shares. Encyclopedias and dictionaries (of philosophers, of sociologists or sociology, of intellectuals, whatever) are and have always been instruments of power and consecration. One of the most common strategies is to include individuals who (according to field-specific criteria) could or should be excluded, or to exclude others who could or should be included. Or again, to modify the structure of the judgments being rendered in this "hit parade," you can put side by side, say, Claude Lévi-Strauss and Bernard-Henri Lévy—that is, someone whose value is indisputable and someone whose value is indisputably disputable. But newspapers intervene as well, posing problems that are then immediately taken up by the journalist-intellectuals. Anti-intellectualism, which is (very understandably) a structural constant in the world of journalism, pushes journalists periodically to impute errors to intellectuals or to initiate debates that will mobilize only other journalist-intellectuals, and frequently often exist only to give these TV intellectuals their media existence.

These external demands are very threatening. In the first place, they can deceive outsiders, who necessarily matter, at least to the extent that cultural producers need listeners, viewers, and readers who buy books and, through sales, affect publishers, and so determine future possibilities of publication. Given the tendency of the media today to celebrate market products designed for the best-seller lists—and their obliging accommodation to backscratching between writer-journalists and journalist-writers—young poets, novelists, sociologists, and historians, who sell three hundred copies of their books are going to have a harder and harder time getting published. I think that, paradoxically, sociology, and most particularly the sociology of intellectuals, has made its own contribution to the state of the French intellectual field today—quite unintentionally, of course. Sociology can in fact be used in two contrary modes. The first, *cynical* mode uses knowledge of the laws of a given milieu to maximize the effect of one's own strategies; the other, which can be called *clinical*, uses the knowledge of these laws or tendencies in order to challenge them. My conviction is that a certain number of cynics—the prophets of transgression, TV's "fast-thinkers," the historian-journalists who edit encyclopedias or spout summaries of contemporary thought—deliberately use sociology (or what they think is sociology) to engineer coups d'état within the intellectual field. You could say as much about the genuinely critical thought of Guy Debord. Touted as the great thinker of the "society of the spectacle," today Debord is used to vindicate a fake, cynical radicalism that ends up cancelling out his thought altogether.

COLLABORATION

But journalistic forces and manipulation can also act more subtly. Like the Trojan horse, they introduce heteronomous agents into autonomous worlds. Supported by external forces, these agents are accorded an authority they cannot get from their peers. These writers for nonwriters or philosophers for nonphilosophers and the like, have television value, a journalistic weight that is not commensurate with their particular weight in their particular world. It's a fact: in certain disciplines, media credentials are now taken more and more into account—even in the review committees of the Centre National de la Recherche Scientifique. Any producer of a TV or radio program who invites a researcher on to a show gives that individual a form of recognition that, until quite recently, was taken as a sign of corruption or decline. Barely thirty years ago, Raymond Aron was seen as deeply suspect, in spite of his hardly debatable merits as a scholar, simply because he was associated with the media as a columnist for *Le Figaro*.[16] Today, the power relationships between fields have changed to the extent that, more and more, external criteria of evaluation—appearing on Bernard Pivot's popular TV book show,[17] being endorsed or profiled by the weekly news magazines—are more important than peer evaluation. This occurs even in the purest universe of the hard sciences. (It would be more complicated for the social sciences because sociologists talk about the social world, in which everyone has a stake and an interest, which means that people have their good and bad sociologists for reasons that have nothing to do with sociology.) In the case of apparently more independent disciplines, such as history or anthropology, biology or physics, media mediation becomes more and more important to the degree that subsidies and grants may depend on a notoriety in which one is hard put to distinguish what is owed to media validation from what is due to peer evaluation. This may seem excessive. Unfortunately, however, I could give all kinds of examples of media intrusion—or, rather the intrusion of economic pressures as relayed by the media—even in the "purest" science. This is why the question of deciding whether or not to appear on television is absolutely central, and why I'd like the scientific community to think about it carefully. Such reflection could increase awareness of the mechanisms I have described, and perhaps could even lead to collective attempts to protect the autonomy crucial to scientific progress against the growing power of television.

For the media to exert power on worlds such as science, the field in question must be complicitous. Sociology enables us to understand this complicity. Journalists often take great satisfaction in noting how eagerly academics rush into the arms of the media, soliciting book reviews and begging for invitations to talk shows, all the while protesting against the oblivion to which they are relegated. Listening to their stories, one comes to have real doubts about the subjective autonomy of writers, artists, and scholars. This dependence has to be put on record. Above all, we must attempt to understand its reasons, or its causes. In some sense, we are seeking to understand who collaborates. I use this word advisedly. A recent issue of the *Actes de la recherche en sciences sociales* contained an article by

Gisèle Sapiro on the French literary field during the Occupation. The goal of this fine analysis was not to say who was or was not a collaborator, nor was it a retrospective settling of accounts; rather, working from a certain number of variables, it attempted to understand why, at a given moment, writers chose one camp and not another. In short, her analysis shows that the more people are recognized by their peers, and are therefore rich in specific capital, the more likely they are to resist. Conversely, the more heteronomous they are in their literary practices, meaning drawn to market criteria (like Claude Farrère, a best-selling author of exotic novels at the time, whose counterparts are easily found today), the more inclined they are to collaborate.

But I have to explain better what "autonomous" means. A highly autonomous field, mathematics for example, is one in which producers' sole consumers are their competitors, that is, individuals who could have made the discovery in question. (I dream of sociology becoming like this, but, unfortunately, everyone wants to get in on the act. Everybody thinks they know what sociology is, and Alain Peyrefitte thinks he has to give me sociology lessons.[18] Well, why not? you may ask, since there are plenty of sociologists or historians only too happy to talk things over with him . . . on television . . .). Autonomy is achieved by constructing a sort of "ivory tower" inside of which people judge, criticize, and even fight each other, but with the appropriate weapons—properly scientific instruments, techniques, and methods. I happened to be on the radio one day with one of my colleagues in history. Right on the air, he says to me, "my dear colleague, I redid your factor analysis (a method of statistic analysis) for the managers, and I didn't get at all what you got." And I thought, "Terrific! Finally, here's someone who is really criticizing me . . ." But it turned out that he'd used a different definition of management and had eliminated bank directors from the population under study. All that had to be done to bring us together was to restore the bank directors (a choice that entailed important theoretical and historical choices). The point is, true scientific agreement or disagreement requires a high degree of agreement about the bases for disagreement and about the means to decide the question. People are sometimes astonished to see on television that historians don't always agree with each other. They don't understand that very often these discussions bring together individuals who have nothing in common and who have no reason even to be talking with one another (somewhat as if you brought together—in just the sort of encounter bad journalists love—an astronomer and an astrologist, a chemist and an alchemist, or a sociologist of religion and a religious cult leader).

From the choices made by French writers under the Occupation can be derived a more general law: The more a cultural producer is autonomous, rich in specific capital from a given field and exclusively integrated into the restricted market in which the only audience is competitors, the greater the inclination to resist. Conversely, the more producers aim for the mass market (like some essayists, writer-journalists, and popular novelists), the more likely they are to collaborate with the powers that be—State, Church, or Party, and, today, journalism and television—and to yield to their demands or their orders.

This law also applies to the present. The objection will be raised that collaborating with the media is not at all the same thing as collaborating with the Nazis. That's true, of course, and obviously, I do not condemn out of hand every kind of collaboration with newspapers, radio, or television. But, from the viewpoint of factors inclining the individual to collaboration, understood as unconditional submission to pressures destructive of the norms of autonomous fields, the analogy is striking. If the fields of science, politics, or literature are threatened by the power of the media, it's because of the presence within them of "heteronomous individuals," people from the outside who have little authority from the viewpoint of the values specific to the field. To use the language of everyday life, these people are already, or are about to become, "failures," which means that they have an interest in heteronomy. It is in their interest to look outside the field for their authority and the rewards (however precipitate, premature, and ephemeral) they did not get inside the field. Moreover, journalists think well of these individuals because they aren't afraid (as they are of more autonomous authors) of people who are ready to accept whatever is required of them. If it seems to me indispensable to combat these heteronomous intellectuals, it's because they constitute the Trojan horse through which heteronomy—that is, the laws of the market and the economy—is brought into the field.

The political field itself enjoys a certain autonomy. Parliament, for example, is an arena within which, in accordance with certain rules, debate and votes resolve disputes between individuals who supposedly articulate divergent or even antagonistic interests. Television produces in this field effects analogous to those it produces in other fields, the juridical field in particular. It challenges the rights of the field to autonomy. To show this mechanism at work, let us examine a story reported in the same issue of *Actes de la recherche en sciences sociales* on the power of journalism, the story of Karine. Karine is a little girl in the south of France who was murdered. The local newspaper reported all the facts, the indignant protests of her father and her uncle, who organized small, local demonstrations, which were carried first by one paper, then a whole string of papers. Everyone said, "How awful! a little kid! We have to reinstate the death penalty." Local political leaders, people close to the National Front, got especially worked up.[19] A conscientious journalist from Toulouse tried to issue a warning: "Watch out! This is a lynching. Take your time, think about what you're doing." Lawyers' groups got involved, denouncing the appeal to vigilante justice . . . Pressure mounted, and when things finally settled down, life imprisonment without parole had been reinstated.

This film run fast forward shows clearly how a perverse

form of direct democracy can come into play when the media act in a way that is calculated to mobilize the public. Such "direct democracy" maximizes the effect both of the pressures working upon the media and of collective emotion. The usual buffers (not necessarily democratic) against these pressures are linked to the relative autonomy of the political field. Absent this autonomy, we are left with a revenge model, precisely the model against which the juridical and even political model of justice was established in the first place. It happens on occasion that, unable to maintain the distance necessary for reflection, journalists end up acting like the fireman who sets the fire. They help create the event by focusing on a story (such as the murder of one young Frenchman by another young man, who is just as French but "of African origin"), and then denounce everyone who adds fuel to the fire that they lit themselves. In this case, I am referring, of course, to the National Front which, obviously, exploits or tries to exploit "the emotions aroused by events." This in the words of the very newspapers and talk shows that startled the whole business by writing the headlines in the first place, and by rehashing events endlessly at the beginning of every evening news program. The media then appear virtuous and humane for denouncing the racist moves of the very figure [LePen] they helped create and to whom they continue to offer his most effective instruments of manipulation.

ENTRY FEE AND EXIT DUTY

I'd now like to say a few words about the relations between esotericism and elitism. This has been a problem since the nineteenth century. Mallarmé, for example—the very symbol of the esoteric, a pure writer, writing for a few people in language unintelligible to ordinary mortals—was concerned throughout his whole life with giving back what he had mastered through his work as a poet. If the media today had existed in full force at the time, he would have wondered: "Shall I appear on TV? How can I reconcile the exigency of 'purity' inherent in scientific and intellectual work, which necessarily leads to esotericism, with the democratic interest in making these achievements available to the greatest number?" Earlier, I pointed out two effects of television. On the one hand, it lowers the "entry fee" in a certain number of fields—philosophical, juridical, and so on. It can designate a sociologist, writer, or philosopher people who haven't paid their dues from the viewpoint of the internal definition of the profession. On the other hand, television has the capacity to reach the greatest number of individuals. What I find difficult to justify is the fact that the extension of the audience is used to legitimate the lowering of the standards for entry into the field. People may object to this as elitism, a simple defense of the besieged citadel of big science and high culture, or even, an attempt to close out ordinary people (by trying to close off television to those who, with their honoraria and showy lif-estyles, claim to be representatives of ordinary men and women, on the pretext that they can be understood by these people and will get high audience ratings). In fact, I am defending the conditions necessary for the production and diffusion of the highest human creations. To escape the twin traps of elitism or demagogy we must work to maintain, even to raise the requirements for the *right of entry*—the entry fee—into the fields of production. I have said that this is what I want for sociology, a field that suffers from the fact that the entry fee is too low—and we must reinforce the *duty to get out,* to share what we have found, while at the same time improving the conditions and the means for doing so.

Someone is always ready to brandish the threat of "leveling" (a recurrent theme of reactionary thought found, for one example, in the work of Heidegger). Leveling can in fact come from the intrusion of media demands into the fields of cultural production. It is essential to defend both the inherent esotericism of all cutting-edge research and the necessity of deesotericizing the esoteric. We must struggle to achieve both these goals under good conditions. In other words, we have to defend the conditions of production necessary for the progress of the universal, while working to generalize the conditions of access to that universality. The more complex an idea—because it has been produced in an autonomous world—the more difficult it is to present to the larger world. To overcome this difficulty, producers in their little citadels have to learn how to get out and fight collectively for optimum conditions of diffusion and for ownership of the relevant means of diffusion. This struggle has to take place as well with teachers, with unions, volontary associations, and so on, so that those on the receiving end receive an education aimed at raising their level of reception. The founders of the French Republic in the late nineteenth century used to say something that is forgotten all too often: The goal of teaching is not only the reading, writing, and arithmetic needed to make a good worker; the goal of education is to offer the means of becoming a good citizen, of putting individuals in a position to understand the law, to understand and to defend their rights, to set up unions . . . We must work to universalize the conditions of access to the universal.

The audience rating system can and should be contested in the name of democracy. This appears paradoxical, because those who defend audience ratings claim that nothing is more democratic (this is a favorite argument of advertisers, which has been picked up by certain sociologists, not to mention essayists who've run out of ideas and are happy to turn any criticism of opinion polls—and audience ratings—into a criticism of universal suffrage). You must, they declare, leave people free to judge and to choose for themselves ("all those elitist intellectual prejudices of yours make you turn your nose up at all this"). The audience rating system is the sanction of the market and the economy, that is, of an external and purely market law. Submission to the requirements of this marketing instrument is the exact equivalent for culture of what poll-based demagogy is for politics. Enslaved by audience ratings, television imposes market pressures on the supposedly free and enlightened consumer. These pressures have nothing to do with the democratic expression of enlightened collective opinion or public rationality, despite what certain commentators would have us believe. The failure of critical thinkers and organizations charged with articulating the interests of dominated individuals to think clearly about this problem only reinforces the mechanisms I have described.

THE POWER OF JOURNALISM[1]

My objective here is not "the power of journalists"—and still less of journalism as a "fourth estate"—but, rather, the hold that the *mechanisms* of a journalistic field increasingly subject to market demands (through readers and advertisers) have *first on journalists* (and on journalist-intellectuals) and then, in part through them, on the various fields of cultural production— the juridical field, the literary field, the artistic field, and the scientific field. Accordingly, we must examine how the structural pressure exerted by the journalistic field, itself dominated by market pressures, more or less profoundly modifies power relationships within other fields. This pressure affects what is done and produced in given fields, with very similar results within these otherwise very different worlds. We must avoid, however, falling into one or the other of two opposite errors: the illusion of the "never-been-seen-before" and its counterpart, "the-way-it-always-has-been."

The power exerted by the journalistic field, and through it the market, on other fields of cultural production, even the most autonomous among them, is not radically new. It wouldn't be difficult to find nineteenth-century texts describing similar effects of the market on these protected worlds.[2] But it is essential not to overlook the specificity of the current situation, which, while in some ways homologous to past situations, is characterized by elements that are indeed new. In their intensity and scope, the effects television produces in the journalistic field and through it, on all other fields of cultural production, are incomparably more significant than those of the rise of so-called industrial literature—with the mass press and the serial novel—which roused nineteenth-century writers to indignation or revolt and led, according to Raymond Williams, to modern definitions of "culture."[3]

The journalistic fields brings to bear on the different fields of

cultural production a group of effects whose form and potency
are linked to its own structure, that is, to the position of the
various media and journalists with respect to their autonomy
vis-à-vis external forces, namely, the twin markets of readers
and advertisers. The degree of autonomy of a news medium is
no doubt measured by the percentage of income that it derives
from advertising and state subsidies (whether indirectly
through program promotion or direct subvention) and also by
the degree of concentration of its advertisers. As for the autonomy of an individual journalist, it depends first of all on the
degree to which press ownership is concentrated. (Concentration of the press augments job insecurity by reducing the number of potential employers.) Next, the individual journalist's
autonomy depends on the position occupied by his newspaper
within the larger space of newspapers, that is, its specific location between the "intellectual" and the "market" poles.
Then, the journalist's own position within that newspaper or
news medium (as reporter, freelancer, and so forth) determines
statutory guarantees (largely a function of reputation) as well
as salary (which makes the individual less vulnerable to the
"soft" forms of public relations and less dependent on writing
for money, potboilers and the like—both of which essentially
relay the financial interests of sponsors). Finally, the journalist's own capacity for autonomous production of news must be
taken into account. (Certain writers, such as popularizers of
science or economic journalists, are in a state of particular
dependence). It is clear that the authorities, the government in
particular, influence the media not only through the economic
pressure that they bring to bear but also through their monopoly on legitimate information—government sources are
the most obvious example. First of all, this monopoly provides
governmental authorities (juridical, scientific, and other authorities as much as the police) with weapons for manipulating
the news or those in charge of transmitting it. For its part, the
press attempts to manipulate these "sources" in order to get a
news exclusive. And we must not ignore the exceptional sym-

bolic power given to state authorities to define, by their actions, their decisions, and their entry into the journalistic field
(interviews, press conferences, and so on), the journalistic
agenda and the hierarchy of importance assigned to events.

SOME CHARACTERISTICS OF THE JOURNALISTIC FIELD

The journalistic field tends to reinforce the "commercial" elements at the core of all fields to the detriment of the "pure." It
favors those cultural producers most susceptible to the seduc-
tions of economic and political powers, at the expense of those
intent on defending the principles and the values of their professions. To understand how this happens, it is necessary to see
that the whole journalistic field is structured like other fields,
and also that market weighs much more heavily on it than on
other fields.

The journalistic field emerged as such during the nineteenth
century around the opposition between newspapers offering
"news," preferably "sensational" or better yet, capable of cre-
ating a sensation, and newspapers featuring analysis and
"commentary," which marked their difference from the other
group by loudly proclaiming the values of "objectivity."[4]
Hence, this field is the site of an opposition between two mod-
els, each with its own principle of legitimation: that of peer
recognition, accorded individuals who internalize most completely the internal "values" or principles of the field; or that
of recognition by the public at large, which is measured by
numbers of readers, listeners, or viewers, and therefore, in the
final analysis, by sales and profits. (Considered from this point
of view, a political referendum expresses the verdict of the
market.)

Like the literary field or the artistic field, then, the journalistic field is the site of a specific, and specifically cultural, model
that is imposed on journalists through a system of overlapping
constraints and the controls that each of these brings to bear

on the others. It is respect for these constraints and controls (sometimes termed a code of ethics) that establishes reputations of professional morality. In fact, outside perhaps the "pick-ups" (when one's work is picked up by another journalist), the value and meaning of which depend on the positions within the field of those who do the taking up and those who benefit from it, there are relatively few indisputable positive sanctions. And negative sanctions, against individuals who fail to cite their sources for example, are practically nonexistent. Consequently, there is a tendency not to cite a journalistic source, especially from a minor news medium, except when necessary to clear one's name.

But, like the political and economic fields, and much more than the scientific, artistic, literary, or juridical fields, the journalistic field is permanently subject to trial by market, whether directly, through advertisers, or indirectly, through audience ratings (even if government subsidies offer a certain independence from immediate market pressures). Furthermore, journalists are no doubt all the more inclined to adopt "audience rating" standards in the production process ("keep it simple," "keep it short") or when evaluating products and even producers ("that's just made for TV," "this will go over really well"), to the extent that those who better represent these standards occupy higher positions (as network heads or editors-in-chief) in news media more directly dependent on the market (that is, commercial television as opposed to PBS). Conversely, younger and less established journalists are more inclined to invoke the principles and values of the "profession" against the more "realistic," or more cynical, stipulations of their "elders."[5]

In the case of a field oriented toward the production of such a highly perishable good as the news, competition for consumers tends to take the form of competition for the newest news ("scoops"). This is increasingly the case, obviously, the closer one gets to the market pole. Market pressure is exercised only through the effect of the field: actually, a high proportion of the

scoops so avidly sought in the battle for customers is destined
to remain unknown as such to readers or viewers. Only competitors will see them, since journalists are the only ones who
read all the newspapers . . . Imprinted in the field's structure
and operating mechanisms, this competition for priority calls
for and favors professionals inclined to place the whole practice of journalism under the sign of speed (or haste) and permanent renewal.[6] This inclination is continually reinforced by
the temporality of journalistic practice, which assigns value to
news according to how new it is (or how "catchy"). This pace
favors a sort of permanent amnesia, the negative obverse of the
exaltation of the new, as well as a propensity to judge producers and products according to the opposition between "new"
or "out-of-date."[7]

Another effect of competition on the field, one that is completely paradoxical and utterly inimical to the assertion of either collective or individual autonomy, is the permanent
surveillance (which can turn into mutual espionage) to which
journalists subject their competitors' activities. The object is to
profit from competitors' failures by avoiding their mistakes,
and to counter their successes by trying to borrow the *supposed* instruments of that success, such as themes for special
issues that "must" be taken up again, books reviewed elsewhere that "you can't not talk about," guests you "must
have," subjects that "have to be covered" because others dis-
covered them, and even big-name journalists who have to appear. This "borrowing" is a result as much of a determination
to keep competitors from having these things as from any real
desire to have them. So here, as in other areas, rather than
automatically generating originality and diversity, competition
tends to favor *uniformity*. This can easily be verified by com-
paring the contents of the major weekly magazines, or radio
and television stations aimed at a general audience. But this
very powerful mechanism also has the effect of insidiously
imposing on the field as a whole the "choices" of those instruments of diffusion most directly and most completely subject

to the market, like television. This, in turn, means that all production is oriented toward preserving established values. This conservatism can be seen, for example, in the way that the periodic "hit parades"—through which journalist-intellectuals try to impose their vision of the field (and, via mutual "back-scratching," gain and confer peer recognition . . .)—almost always feature the authors of highly perishable cultural goods; these goods are nonetheless destined, with the help of the media, for the best-seller list, along with authors recognized both as a "sure value," capable of validating the good taste of those who validate them, and as best-sellers in the long run. Which is to say that even if the actors have an effect as individuals, it is the *structure* of the journalistic field that determines the intensity and orientation of its mechanisms, as well as their effects on other fields.

THE EFFECTS OF INTRUSION

In every field, the influence of the journalistic field tends to favor those actors and institutions closer to the market. This effect is all the stronger in fields that are themselves structurally more tightly subordinated to this market model, as well as wherever the journalistic field exercising this power is also more subordinated to those external pressures that have a structurally stronger effect on it than on other fields of cultural production. But we see today that internal sanctions are losing their symbolic force, and that "serious" journalists and newspapers are also losing their cachet as they suffer under the pressure to make concessions to the market, to the marketing tactics introduced by commercial television, and to the new principle of legitimacy based on ratings and "visibility." These things, marketing and media visibility, become the—seemingly more democratic—substitute for the internal standards by which specialized fields once judged cultural and even political products and their producers. Certain "analyses" of television

owe their popularity with journalists—especially those most
susceptible to the effects of audience ratings—to the fact that
they confer a *democratic legitimacy* to the market model by
posing in *political* terms (as, for example, a referendum), what
is a problem of *cultural* production and diffusion.[8]

Thus, the increased power of a journalistic field itself increasingly subject to direct or indirect domination by the market model threatens the autonomy of other fields of cultural
production. It does so by supporting those actors or enterprises
at the very core of these fields that are most inclined to yield to
the seduction of "external" profits precisely because they are
less rich in capital specific to the field (scientific, literary, or
other) and therefore less assured of the specific rewards the
field is in a position to guarantee in the short or longer term.

The journalistic field exercises power over other fields of
cultural production (especially philosophy and the social sciences) primarily through the intervention of cultural producers
located in an uncertain site between the journalistic field and
the specialized fields (the literary or philosophical, and so on).
These journalist-intellectuals use their dual attachments to
evade the requirements specific to each of the worlds they
inhabit, importing into each the capabilities they have more or
less completely acquired in the other. In so doing, they exercise
two major effects.[9] On the one hand, they introduce new forms
of cultural production, located in a poorly defined intermedi-
ary position between academic esotericism and journalistic
"exotericism." On the other hand, particularly through their
critical assessments, they impose on cultural products evaluative principles that validate market sanctions by giving them a
semblance of intellectual authority and reinforcing the spontaneous inclination of certain categories of consumers to *allodoxia*. So that, by orienting choices (editors' choices, for one)
toward the least demanding and most commercially viable
products, these journalist-intellectuals reinforce the impact of
audience ratings or the best-seller list on the reception of cul-

tural products and ultimately if indirectly, on cultural production itself.[10]

Moreover, they can count on the support of those who equate "objectivity" with a sort of social savoir-vivre and an eclectic neutrality with respect to all parties concerned. This group puts middlebrow cultural products in the avant-garde or denigrates avant-garde work (and not only in art) in the name of common sense. But this group in its turn can count on the approval or even the complicity of consumers who, like them, are inclined to *allodoxia* by their distance from the "center of cultural values" and by their self-interested propensity to hide from themselves the limits of their own capacities of appropriation—following the model of self-deception that is expressed so well by readers of popularizing journals when they assert that "this is a high-level scientific journal that anybody can understand."

In this way, achievements made possible by the autonomy of the field and by its capacity to resist social demands can be threatened. It was with these dynamics in mind, symbolized today by audience ratings, that writers in the last century objected vehemently to the idea that art (the same could be said of science) should be subject to the judgments of universal suffrage. Against this threat there are two possible strategies, more or less frequently adopted according to the field and its degree of autonomy. One may firmly delimit the field and endeavor to restore the borders threatened by the intrusion of journalistic modes of thought and action. Alternatively, one may quit the ivory tower (following the model Émile Zola inaugurated during the Dreyfus Affair) to impose the values nurtured in that tower and to use all available means, within one's specialized field and without, and also within the journalistic field itself, to try to impose on the outside the achievements and victories that autonomy made possible.

There are economic and cultural conditions of access to enlightened scientific judgment. There can be no recourse to universal suffrage (or opinion polls) to decide properly scientific problems (even though this is sometimes done indirectly, with no one the wiser) without annihilating the very conditions of scientific production, that is, the entry barrier that protects the scientific (or artistic) world against the destructive invasion of external, therefore inappropriate and misplaced, principles of production and evaluation. But it should not be concluded that the barrier cannot be crossed *in the other direction*, or that it is intrinsically impossible to work for a democratic redistribution of the achievements made possible by autonomy—on the condition that it clearly be seen that every action aimed at disclosing the rarest achievements of the most advanced scientific or artistic work assumes a challenge to the *monopoly of the instruments of diffusion* of this scientific or artistic information, that is, to the monopoly held by the journalistic field. We must also question the representation of the general public's expectations as constructed by the market demagogy of those individuals in a position to set themselves between cultural producers (today, this applies to politicians as well) and the great mass of consumers (or voters).

The distance between professional cultural producers (or their products) and ordinary consumers (readers, listeners, or viewers, and voters as well) relates to the autonomy of the field in question and varies according to field. It will be greater or lesser, more or less difficult to cross, and more or less unacceptable from the point of view of democratic principles. And, contrary to appearances, this distance also exists in politics, whose declared principles it contradicts. Like those in the journalistic field, actors in the political field are in a competitive relationship of continual struggle. Indeed, in a certain way, the journalistic field is part of the political field on which it has such a powerful impact. Nevertheless, these two fields are both very directly and very tightly in the grip of the market and the referendum. It follows that the power wielded by the journalistic field reinforces the tendencies of political actors to accede to the expectations and the demands of the largest majority. Because these demands are sometimes highly emotional and unreflective, their articulation by the press often turns them into claims capable of mobilizing groups.

Except when it makes use of the freedoms and critical powers assured by autonomy, the press, especially the televised (commercial) press, acts in the same way as polls (with which it, too, has to contend). While polls can serve as an instrument of rationalistic demagogy which tends to reinforce the self enclosure of the political field, their primary function is to set up a direct relationship with voters, a relationship *without mediation* which eliminates from the game all individual or collective actors (such as political parties or unions) socially mandated to elaborate and propose considered solutions to social questions. This unmediated relationship takes away from all self-styled spokesmen and delegates the claim (made in the past by all the great newspaper editors) to a monopoly on legitimate expression of "public opinion." At the same time, it deprives them of their ability to elaborate critically (and sometimes collectively, as in legislative assemblies) their constituents' actual or assumed will.

For all of these reasons, the ever-increasing power of a journalistic field itself increasingly subject to the power of the market model to influence a political field haunted by the temptation of demagogy (most particularly at a time when polls offer the means for a rationalized exercise of demagogic action) weakens the autonomy of the political field. It weakens as well the powers accorded representatives (political and other) as a function of their competence as *experts* or their authority as *guardians of collective values.*

Finally, how can one not point to the judges who, at the price of a "pious hypocrisy," are able to perpetuate the belief that their decisions are based not in external, particularly economic constraints, but in the transcendent norms of which they are the guardians? The juridical field is not what it thinks it is. It is not a pure world, free of concessions to politics or the economy. But its image of purity produces absolutely real social effects, first of all, on the very individuals whose job it is to declare the law. But what would happen to judges, understood as the more or less sincere incarnations of a collective hypocrisy, if it became widely accepted that, far from obeying transcendent, universal verities and values, they are thoroughly subject, like all other social actors, to constraints such as those placed on them, irrespective of judicial procedures and hierarchies, by the pressures of economic necessity or the seduction of media success?

APPENDIX

The Olympics—An Agenda for Analysis[1]

What exactly do we mean when we talk about the Olympics? The apparent referent is what "really" happens. That is to say, the gigantic spectacle of sport in which athletes from all over the world compete under the sign of universalistic ideals; as well as the markedly national, even patriotic ritual of the parades by various national teams, and the award ceremonies replete with flying flags and blaring anthems. But the hidden referent is the television show, the ensemble of representations of the first spectacle, as it is filmed and broadcast by television in selections which, since the competition is international, appear unmarked by national bias. The Olympics, then, are doubly hidden: no one sees all of it, and no one sees that they don't see it. Every television viewer can have the illusion of seeing *the* (real) Olympics.

It may seem simply to record events as they take place, but in fact, given that each national television network gives more airplay to athletes or events that satisfy national pride, television transforms a sports competition between athletes from all over into a confrontation between champions, that is, officially selected competitors from different countries.

To understand this process of symbolic transformation, we would first have to analyze the social construction of the entire Olympic spectacle. We'd have to look at the individual events and at everything that takes place around them, such as the opening and closing parades. Then we'd have to look at the production of the televised image of this spectacle. Inasmuch as it is a prop for advertising, the televised event is a commercial, marketable product that must be designed to reach the largest audience and hold on to it the longest. Aside from the fact that these events must be timed to be shown on prime time in economically dominant countries, these programs must be tailored to meet audience demand. The expectations of different national publics and their preferences for one or another sport have to be taken into account. The sports given prominence and the individual games or meets shown must be carefully selected to showcase the national teams most likely to win events and thereby gratify national pride. It follows that the relative importance of the different sports within the international sports organizations increasingly depends on their television popularity and the correlated financial return they promise. More and more, as well, the constraints of television broadcasting influence the choice of sports included in Olympic competition, the site and time slot awarded to each sport, and even the ways in which matches and ceremonies take place. This is why (after negotiations structured by tremendous financial considerations), the key final events at the Seoul Olympics were scheduled to coincide with prime time in the United States.

All of which means that to understand the games, we would have to look at the whole field of production of the Olympics as a *televised show* or, in marketing terms, as a "means of communication." That is to say, we would have to assess all the objective relations between the agents and institutions competing to produce and sell the images of, and commentary about, the Olympics. These would include first the International Olympic Committee (IOC), which has gradually become a vast commercial enterprise with an annual budget of $20 million, dominated by a small, closed group of sports executives and representatives from major companies (Adidas, Coca-Cola, and so on). The IOC controls transmission rights (which were estimated, for Barcelona, at $633 billion), sponsorship rights, and the Olympic city selection. Second, we would need to turn our attention to the big (especially American) television networks competing for transmission rights (divided up by country or by language). Third would be the large multinational corporations (Coca-Cola, Kodak, Ricoh, Phillips, and so on) competing for exclusive world rights to promote their products in connection with the Games (as "official sponsors").[2] Finally, we cannot forget the producers of images and commentary for television, radio, and newspapers (some ten thousand at Barcelona), since it is their competition that conditions the construction of the representation of the Olympics by influencing how these images are selected, framed, and edited, and how the commentary is elaborated. Another important consideration is the intensified competition between countries that is produced by the globalization of the Olympic spectacle. The effects of this competition can be seen in official *sports policies* to promote international sports success, maximizing the symbolic and financial rewards of victory and resulting in the *industrialization of the production of sports* that implies the use of drugs and authoritarian forms of training.[3]

A parallel can be seen in artistic production. The individual artist's directly visible actions obscure the activity of the other actors—critics, gallery owners, museum curators, and so on—who, in and through their competition, collaborate to produce the meaning and the value of both the artwork and the artist. Even more important, they produce the very belief in the value of art and the artist that is the basis of the whole art game.[4] Likewise, in sports, the champion runner or javelin thrower is only the obvious subject of a spectacle that in some sense is produced twice.[5] The first production is the actual event in the stadium, which is put together by a whole array of actors, including athletes, trainers, doctors, organizers, judges, goalkeepers, and masters of the ceremonies. The second show reproduces the first in images and commentary. Usually laboring under enormous pressure, those who produce on the second show are caught up in a whole network of objective relationships that weighs heavily on each of them.

As a collectivity, the participants in the event we call "the Olympics" might conceivably come to control the mechanisms that affect them all. But they would be able to do so only by undertaking a serious investigation to bring to light the mechanisms behind this *two-step social construction,* first of the sports event, then of the media event. Only with the conscious control of these mechanisms that can be gained from such a process of research and reflection would this collectivity be able to maximize the potential for universalism—today in danger of extinction—that is contained within the Olympic Games.[6]

TRANSLATOR'S NOTE

As Pierre Bourdieu explains, this work aims at an audience beyond the usual public for his scholarly works. To make connections to the French situation, for the most part all Anglo-American readers need do is follow Bourdieu's reasoning, supplying their own equivalents from Britain or the U.S. or, indeed, elsewhere. However, an important element that needs to be mentioned because it is absent from American or British journalism is the extent to which the government intervenes in the operations of all media.[1] A ministry of communication (grouped for some administrations with the ministry of culture) oversees the direct or indirect financial support accorded the print press, radio, and television, regulates their competition, and determines as well the nature and kind of official information made available. (The Service juridique et technique de l'information, which reports directly to the prime minister, is charged with coordinating communications policy and subventions.) Forms of support range from direct subsidies, tax reductions, and postal benefits to promotional campaigns for one or another official policy which are paid for by the government. It is not unheard of for total governmental support to reach 20 percent of income for a newspaper or journal. The goal of this financial intervention is to guarantee economic viability of "serious" opinion journals and reviews by removing them from the hold of the market. Similarly, the governmental supports the production of French television programs by limiting the proportion of foreign (read, American) programs that may be broadcast. (A few years ago, this protectionism brought France into direct conflict with the U.S. during the negotiations of GATT [General Agreement on Tariffs and Trade].)

Television in particular is subject to governmental controls. The first three television networks, established in 1949 (TF1),

1964 (Antenne 2), and 1973 (FR3, a regional network), were until recently almost entirely government subsidized and run. Originally absent altogether, advertising was introduced with two minutes per day in 1970, which had become twenty minutes a decade later, and increasingly prominent since. Liberalization of radio and television received its big push in the Events of 1968, when the ORTF (Office de la Radio et Télévision Françaises) went on strike. By the 1980s, begun by Valéry Giscard d'Estaing but primarily under the Socialist François Mitterrand, the government monopoly on programming was eliminated, a cable station was added (Canal Plus), TF1 and La Cinq were privatized, M6 and 7 were created; Channel 7 eventually turned into Arte, which, as its name suggests, is devoted to more or less high-cultural fare, not unlike but of a higher level than public broadcasting stations in the United States.

A further distinction, notably from the American press, is the strongly defined political orientations claimed and proclaimed by the print media in France. The principal national dailies referred to in *On Television* are *Libération* (center-left), *Le Monde* (center-liberal), *Le Figaro* (right-conservative), *L'Humanité* (the paper of the French Communist Party), and tabloids like *France-Soir*. The prominent weekly news magazines on the order of *Time* or *Newsweek* are *L'Express* (center) and *Le Nouvel Observateur* (center-left). *Le Monde diplomatique*, a monthly journal devoted to foreign affairs, represents liberal (in the Anglo-American sense) currents of reflection. The National Front, the radical right party led by Jean-Marie LePen (whom Bourdieu targets in Part Two of *On Television*), has no comparable news outlet.

As far as official institutions goes, it is not irrelevant that Pierre Bourdieu himself speaks from and with the authority of a peculiarly French institution, the Collège de France, founded in 1543 to counter the conservatism of the Sorbonne. The Collège grants no degrees and gives the professors (who are elected by the other members) exceptional freedom to pursue their research and an especially public venue to present that research. (All lectures are free and open to the public). Prominent scholars at the Collège have included Louis Pasteur, Henri Bergson, and Marcel Mauss, and closer to the present, Raymond Aron, Michel Foucault, Roland Barthes, and Claude Lévi-Strauss. Bourdieu was elected to a chair in sociology in 1980.

BIBLIOGRAPHY

Accardo, Alain, with G. Abou, G. Balastre, and D. Matine. *Journalistes au quotidien: outils pour une socioanalyse des pratiques journalistiques.* Bordeaux: Mascaret, 1995.

Accardo, Alain. "Academic destiny," pp. 719–35, in Pierre Bourdieu, et al., *La Misère du monde.* [*Misère*, P. Ferguson et al., trans., Cambridge: Polity Press, forthcoming].

Bourdieu, Pierre. *Distinction: A Social Critique of the Judgment of Taste* [1979] trans. R. Nice. Cambridge: Harvard University Press, 1984.

———. "L'Emprise du journalisme," *Actes de la recherche en sciences sociales* 101–102, March 1994: 3–9.

———. "The Institutionalization of Anomie," pp. 238–53 in *The Field of Cultural Production: Essays on Art and Literature.* Ed. Randal Johnson. New York: Columbia University Press, 1993.

———. *The Rules of Art: Genesis and Structure of the Literary Field.* Trans. S. Emanuel. Stanford: Stanford University Press, 1996.

———. *The State Nobility: Elite Schools in the Field of Power.* Trans. L. Clough. Cambridge: Polity Press, 1996.

———. (with Loïc Wacquant). *An Invitation to Reflexive Sociology.* Chicago: University of Chicago Press, 1992.

Champagne, Patrick. "La Construction médiatique des 'malaises sociaux,'" *Actes de la recherche en sciences sociales* 90, December 1991: 64–75.

———. "La Loi des grands nombres: mesure de l'audience et représentation politique du public," *Actes de la recherche en sciences sociales*, 101–102, March 1994: 10–22.

———. "Le Journalisme entre précarité et concurrence," *Liber* 29, December 1996.

———. "The View from the Media." In Pierre Bourdieu, et al.,

La Misère, trans. P. Ferguson, et al. Cambridge: Polity Press, forthcoming.

Deleuze, Gilles. *A propos des nouveaux philosophes et d'un problème plus général.* Paris: Minuit, 1978.

Fallows, James. *Breaking the News. How the Media Undermine American Democracy.* New York: Vintage, 1997.

Ferenczi, Thomas. *L'Invention du journalisme en France: naissance de la presse moderne à la fin du 19ᵉ siècle.* Paris: Plon, 1993.

Gaarder, Jostein. *Le Monde de Sophie: roman sur l'histoire de la philosophie.* Trans. from the Norwegian by H. Hervieu and M. Laffon. Paris: Seuil, 1995.

Godard, Jean-Luc. "Enquête sur une image." 1972 interview, originally a film entitled "Letter to Jane," pp. 350–362, in *Jean-Luc Godard par Jean-Luc Godard*, ed. Alain Bergala. Paris: Cahiers du cinéma-Éditions de l'Étoile, 1985.

————— "Pour mieux écouter les autres." 1972, interview, pp. 362–367, in *Jean-Luc Godard par Jean-Luc Godard*, ed. Alain Bergala. Paris: Cahiers du cinéma—Éditions de l'Étoile, 1985.

Goulemot, Jean-Marie, and Daniel Oster. *Gens de lettres, Écrivains et bohèmes: L'imaginaire littéraire, 1630–1900.* Paris: Minerve, 1992.

Hoberman, John M. *Mortal Engines: The Science of Performance and the Dehumanization of Sport.* New York: Free Press, 1992.

Homer. *Iliad.* Trans. R. Lattimore. Chicago: University of Chicago Press, 1951.

Lenoir, Remi. "La Parole est aux juges: crise de la magistrature et champ journalistique." *Actes de la recherche en sciences sociales* 101–102, March 1994: 77–84.

Murray, Philippe. "Des Régles de l'art aux coulisses de sa misère." *Art Press* 186, June 1993: 55–67.

Pouthier, Jean-Luc. "L'État et la communication. Le "modèle français," pp. 582–586, in *L'État de la France 95–96.* Paris: La Découverte, 1995.

Sapiro, Gisèle. "La Raison littéraire: le champ littéraire français sous l'Occupation (1940–1944)." *Actes de la recherche en sciences sociales* 111–12, March 1996: 3–35.

——. "Salut littéraire et littérature du salut: deux trajectoires de romanciers catholiques: François Mauriac et Henry Bordeaux." *Actes de la recherche en sciences sociales* 111–12, March 1996: 36–58.

Schudson, Michael. *Discovering the News*. New York: Basic Books, 1978.

Simson, Vyv, and Andrew Jennings. *The Lords of the Rings: Power, Money and Drugs in the Modern Olympics*. London: Simon and Schuster, 1992.

Williams, Raymond. *Culture and Society, 1780–1950*. New York: Columbia University Press, 1958.

Wolton, Dominique. "Culture et télévision: entre cohabitation et apartheid." In *Éloge du grand public: une théorie critique de la télévision*. Paris: Flammarion, 1990.

NOTES

1. To avoid producing "finger-pointing" or caricature (effects easily produced whenever recorded interviews or printed texts are published as is), I have had to leave out documents that would have given my argument all its force and—because highlighting pulls them out of a familiar context—would have reminded the reader of similar examples that ordinary observation fails to see.

2. [*On Television* raised a widespread controversy that lasted several months and engaged the most important journalists and columnists from the daily papers, the weekly news magazines, and the television stations. During this period the book was at the top of the best-seller list.—T.R.]

3. [Pierre Bourdieu et al., *La Misère du monde* (Paris: Seuil, 1993), trans. P. Ferguson et al. (Cambridge: Polity Press, forthcoming). This book contains some seventy interviews with individuals across the spectrum of French society, which are placed within a theoretical, historical, political, and personal context of the interviewer. The work is a multifaceted ethnographic and sociological study by Bourdieu and his team, but it is also a collection of wonderfully evocative (if rather depressing) life stories. It is these narratives that made *La Misère du monde* the best-seller that it became.—T.R.]

4. [*The State Nobility: Elite Schools in the Field of Power*, trans. L. Clough (Cambridge: Polity Press, 1996). The Grandes Écoles are prestigious wholly state-subsidized, nonuniversity schools in a number of areas, including engineering (the École Polytechnique), the humanities and science (the École Normale Supérieure), administration (the École Nationale d'Administration), and commerce (Hautes Études Commerciales). Unlike the universities, which admit students on the basis of their high school diploma (the *baccalauréat* examination), the Grandes Écoles admit students after a highly competitive entrance examination.—T.R.]

5. [*Iliad*, trans. R. Lattimore (Chicago: University of Chicago Press, 1951), 2:212–256.—T.R.]

6. See James Fallows, *Breaking the News: How The Media Undermine American Democracy* (New York: Vintage, 1997).

7. See Patrick Champagne, "Le Journalisme entre précarité et concurrence," *Liber* 29 (Dec. 1996).

NOTES TO PREFACE

1. This text is the revised and corrected unabridged transcription of two television programs that were part of a series of courses from the Collège de France. The shows were taped on March 18, 1996, and shown by the Paris Première station the following May ("On Television" and "The Field of Journalism," Collège de France—CNRS audiovisual production). The appendix reproduces an article from a special issue of the *Actes de la recherche en sciences sociales* [founded by Pierre Bourdieu in 1975] on the power of television, which addresses the themes of these two lectures more rigorously.

2. [Jean-Luc Godard, "Pour Mieux écouter les autres," 1972 interview with Jean-Luc Godard, in *Jean-Luc Godard par Jean-Luc Godard*, ed. Alain Bergala (Paris: Cahiers du cinéma—Editions de l'Etoile, 1985), p. 366. The earlier reference is to Godard's extensive analysis of the political subtexts and uses of the widely diffused photograph of Jane Fonda talking to North Vietnamese. "Enquête sur une image," 1972 interview, originally a film entitled "Letter to Jane," in ibid., pp. 350–362.—T.R.]

NOTES TO PART ONE:
IN FRONT OF THE CAMERA AND BEHIND THE SCENES

1. [Bouygues is the largest French company in commercial and public works construction. The subsidiaries of the holding company cover a wide range of goods and services, including telecommunications. It controls 42 percent of the TF1 television station.—T.R.]

2. ["The View from the Media," in Pierre Bourdieu, et al., *La Misère*. The French "suburbs" [*banlieue*] correspond to the American "inner city," which is the translation used here.

3. [Bourdieu here refers to the controversy in France which began in 1989 when Muslim girls, children of relatively recent immigrants from North Africa, were expelled from public school for wearing headscarves (*le foulard* in French, *le hidjab* in Arabic, sometimes tendentiously translated as "veil"). After much debate the then–Minister of Education Lionel Jospin authorized wearing the scarf in class.—T.R.]

4. [English in the original, as are "fast-thinkers," "talk-show," "news" below.—T.R.]

5. [Jostein Gaarder, *Le Monde de Sophie: roman sur l'histoire de la philosophie* (Paris: Seuil, 1995), translated from the Norwegian by H. Hervieu and M. Laffon, was a curious and phenomenal best-seller, perhaps luring unsuspecting readers by the subtitle that announces a novel instead of an introduction to philosophic thought.—T.R.]

6. [Bourdieu refers to well-known and often-seen political pundits and social commentators, journalists and writers as well as academics, all of whom have written numerous books and have multiiple connections in journalism and publishing. Alain Minc is an industrialist and social commentator closely connected to *Le Monde*; Jacques Attali was a prominent adviser to the Socialist President François Mitterrand; Guy Sorman is a journalist and newspaper editor; Luc Ferry is a professor of philosophy at the University of Caen, who writes regularly for *L'Express*; Alain Finkielkraut is a philosopher who teaches at the École Polytechnique; the historian Jacques Julliard, a regular commentator on the radio station Europe 1, is Director of Studies at the École des Hautes Études en Sciences Sociales [the prestigious, nonuniversity institution for teaching and research in the social sciences where Pierre Bourdieu also holds an appointment], and is associate editor of *Le Nouvel Observateur*; Claude Imbert is the editor of the middle-of-the-road business-oriented news magazine *Le Point*; Nicolas Sarkozy is an important figure in the conservative RPR [Rally for the Republic] party of President Jacques Chirac. Bourdieu cites Jacques Julliard's diary, *L'Année des dupes* (Paris: Seuil, 1996), for an illustration of how the system works.—T.R.]

7. [Guillaume Durand hosts a late-night talk show on TF1.—T.R.]

8. [Since 1990, Jean-Marie Cavada has produced and moderated a talk show on the France 3 television channel. In December 1996 he was appointed as director of the educational channel La Cinquième.

The strike in question was called in November 1995, when the then-conservative prime minister Alain Juppé proposed raising the retirement age for workers on the national railway system. The general railroad strike lasted into December. Juppé eventually withdrew the proposal, leaving the retirement age at fifty.—T.R.]

9. [Television in France developed comparatively late: in 1963, France had some 3 million TV sets against 12 million in Great Britain. It has since caught up so that by 1984 there were television sets in 93 percent of French households and 94 percent of homes in Great Britain.—T.R.]

NOTES TO PART TWO:
INVISIBLE STRUCTURES AND THEIR EFFECTS

10. [See Raymond Williams, *Culture and Society, 1780–1950* (New York: Columbia University Press, 1958).—T.R.]

11. [See Pierre Bourdieu, "The Institutionalization of Anomie," in Randal Johnson, ed., *The Field of Cultural Production: Essays on Art and Literature* (New York: Columbia University Press, 1993), pp. 238–53.—T.R.]

12. For example, the long-running show of Bernard Pivot (see note 17, below). The American equivalents are found on PBS.—T.R.]

13. [The Puppets [*Les Guignols*] is a weekly satirical program where prominent political figures are represented by marionettes with exaggerated features and such.—T.R.]

14. [Bernard-Henri Lévy is one of the most prominent of contemporary journalist-philosophers, so well known in fact that he is often referred simply as "BHL." Besides his many books and essays, he has written plays and directed films (and has acted in television drama). Lévy has also taken a particularly active stand in favor of Bosnia (see his film from 1992, *La Mort de Sarajevo*).—T.R.]

15. [Remi Lenoir, "La Parole est aux juges: crise de la magistrature et champ journalistique," *Actes de la recherche en sciences sociales*, 101–102 (March 1994), pp. 77–84; and Patrick Champagne, "La Loi des grands nombres: mesure de l'audience et représentation politique du public," in ibid., pp. 64–75.—T.R.]

16. [The eminent sociologist and political scientist Raymond Aron (1905–1983) was appointed (in 1958) to the Chair in Sociol-

ogy at the Sorbonne, originally occupied by Émile Durkheim, and elected to the Collège de France in 1970.—T.R.]

17. [From 1975 to 1990, Bernard Pivot was the extraordinarily popular host of *Apostrophes*, a book review show on the Antenne 2 television station. An appearance on this show made reputations and all but guaranteed sales. His current program, on France 2, has a somewhat different format and rather less impact.—T.R.]

18. [Alain Peyrefitte is a well-known writer and essayist, member of the Académie Française, one-time Attorney General of France, who is currently also a columnist for the conservative newspaper *Le Figaro*.—T.R.]

19. [France abolished the death penalty in 1981 under the newly elected Socialist government of François Mitterrand. The National Front is the extreme right-wing party led by Jean-Marie LePen.—T.R.]

NOTES TO THE POWER OF JOURNALISM

1. I thought it useful to reproduce this text, which has already been published in *Les Actes de la recherche en sciences sociales*, in which I had set out, in a more tightly controlled form, most of the themes discussed in a more accessible fashion above.

2. See for example the work of Jean-Marie Goulemot and Daniel Oster, *Gens de lettres: écrivains et bohèmes, l'imaginaire littéraire, 1630–1900* (Paris: Minerve, 1992), which gives numerous examples of observations and remarks by writers themselves that constitute a sort of spontaneous sociology of the literary milieu. They do not, however, derive the basic explanatory principle, largely because of their efforts to objectify their adversaries and everything they dislike about the literary world. But the picture that emerges of the functioning of the nineteenth-century literary field can be read as a description of the concealed or secret functioning of the literary field today (as Philippe Murray has done in "Des Règles de l'art aux coulisses de sa misère," *Art Press* 186 [June 1993], (pp. 55–67).

3. [Raymond Williams, *Culture and Society, 1780–1950* (New York: Columbia University Press, 1958).—T.R.]

4. On the emergence of this idea of "objectivity" in American journalism as a product of the effort of newspapers worried about

their respectability to distinguish news from the simple narrative of the popular press, see Michael Schudson, *Discovering the News* (New York: Basic Books, 1978). On the opposition between journalists oriented toward the literary field and concerned with style, and journalists close to the political field, and on what each contributed, in the French case, to this process of differentiation and the invention of a "job" of its own (notably, with the advent of the reporter), see Thomas Ferenczi, *L'Invention du journalisme en France: naissance de la presse moderne à la fin du 19ᵉ siècle* (Paris: Plon, 1993). On the form that this opposition takes in the field of French newspapers and news magazines and on its relationship with the different categories of reading and readers, see Pierre Bourdieu, *Distinction: A Social Critique of the Judgement of Taste* [1979] trans. R. Nice (Cambridge: Harvard University Press, 1984), pp. 442–51.

5. As with the literary field, the hierarchy that is constructed according to the external criterion—sales—is just about the reverse of that set up by the internal criterion—journalistic "seriousness." The complexity of this structurally chiasmic distribution (which is also the distribution in the literary, artistic, and juridical fields) is redoubled by the fact that, at the heart of print media or television, each one of which functions like a subfield, the opposition between a "cultural" pole and a "market" pole organizes the entire field. The result is a series of structures within structures (type a:b::b1:b2).

6. It is through temporal constraints, often imposed in purely arbitrary fashion, that *structural censorship* is exerted, almost unnoticed, on what may be said by television talk show guests.

7. If the assertion that "it's out-of-date" or "we've gone beyond that" today so often takes the place of critical argument (and this is true well beyond the journalistic field), this is because the rushed actors have an obvious self-interest in putting this evaluative principle to work. It confers an indisputable advantage to the last-in, to the youngest. Further, because it is reducible to something like the virtually empty opposition between "before" and "after," this kind of assertion obviates the need to prove one's case.

8. All that has to be done is to formulate the problems of journalists (like the choice between TF1 and Arte) in terms that could be those of journalism. See Dominique Wolton, "Culture et télévision: entre cohabitation et apartheid," in *Éloge du grand public: une*

théorie critique de la télévision (Paris: Flammarion, 1990), p. 163. In passing, and to justify how rough and even laborious scientific analysis can appear, let me stress the degree to which adequate construction of the analytic object depends on breaking with the preconstructions and presuppositions of everyday language, most particularly with the language of journalism.

9. The uncertain boundaries of "journalist-intellectual" category make it necessary to differentiate those cultural producers who, following a tradition that began with the advent of "industrial" cultural production, ask of the journalistic professions the *means of existence* and rather than powers (of control or validation) capable of acting on the specialized fields (the Zhdanov effect). [Andrei Aleksandrovich Zhdanov (1890–1948), a loyal Stalinist, member of the Politburo, and general in the Finnish-Russian war of 1939–1940. Bourdieu refers to Zhdanov's political control of the intellectuals in the postwar Soviet Union.—T.R.]

10. A number of recent battles over modern art are hardly distinguishable, except perhaps by the pretension of their claims, from the judgments that would be obtained if avant-garde art were put to a referendum or, what comes down to the same thing, to an opinion poll.

NOTES TO THE OLYMPICS — AN AGENDA FOR ANALYSIS

1. This text is an abridged version of a talk given at the 1992 Annual Meeting of the Philosophical Society for the Study of Sport in Berlin, held in Berlin on October 2, 1992. It was subsequently published in the *Actes de la recherche en sciences sociales* 103 (June 1994), pp. 102–103.

2. "Sponsors were offered a complete communication package based on product category exclusivity and continuity over a four-year period. The programme for each of seventy-five matches included stadium advertising, official supplier's titles, the use of mascots and emblems and franchise opportunities." For £7 million [$14 million] each sponsor in 1986 had the possibility of a share of "the biggest single televised event in the world," with "unparalleled exposure, far in excess of other sports" (Vyv Simson and Andrew Jennings, *The*

Lords of the Rings: Power, Money and Drugs in the Modern Olympics [London: Simon and Schuster, 1992], p. 102).

3. The top competitive sports increasingly rely on an industrial technology that calls on various biological and psychological sciences to transform the human body into a efficient and inexhaustible machine. Competition between national teams and governments increasingly and ever-more emphatically encourages the use of prohibited substances and dubious methods of training. See John M. Hoberman, *Mortal Engines: The Science of Performance and the Dehumanization of Sport* (New York: Free Press, 1992).

4. See Pierre Bourdieu, *The Rules of Art: Genesis and Structure of the Literary Field*, trans. S. Emanuel (Stanford, Calif.: Stanford University Press, 1996).

5. For a gross indicator of the real value of different actors of Olympic "show business," the presents distributed by the Korean authorities to different important figures went from $1100 for IOC members to $110 for the athletes. See Simson and Jennings, *Lords of the Rings*, p. 153.

6. One could, for example, imagine an *Olympic charter* that would define the principles to be followed by everyone involved in the production of both shows (beginning, obviously, with the men who run the Olympic Committee, who are the first to benefit from transgressions of financial disinterestedness they are supposed to enforce). Or an Olympic oath could bind the athletes (prohibiting them, for example, from joining in patriotic demonstrations like carrying the national flag once around the stadium) and those who produce and comment on the images of these exploits.

NOTES TO TRANSLATOR'S NOTE

1. See Jean-Luc Pouthier, "L'Etat et la communication; le 'modèle français,'" pp. 582–586 in *L'Etat de la France 95–96* (Paris: La Découverte, 1995).

INDEX

Page references followed by "n." or "nn." refer to information in notes.